# Performance Assessment

## TEACHER'S GUIDE

- INTERVIEW/TASK TESTS
- QUARTERLY EXTENDED PERFORMANCE ASSESSMENTS
  SCORING RUBRICS
  SAMPLE STUDENT PAPERS
  PERFORMANCE INDICATORS
  ANSWER KEYS
- MANAGEMENT FORMS

## Grade 7

Harcourt Brace & Company

Orlando • Atlanta • Austin • Boston • San Francisco • Chicago • Dallas • New York • Toronto • London

*http://www.hbschool.com*

# CONTENTS

**Evaluating Interview/Task Test Items**

▶ **Interview Task/Test and Evaluation Criteria**

# Performance Assessment Program

## Unique Features of Math Advantage Performance Assessment

To create assessments that actually evaluate what is taught, it is necessary to target specific math concepts, skills, and strategies at each grade level. In planning the assessment program for *Math Advantage,* a review was made of performance assessments cited in professional literature and also of those used in state testing programs. Comparisons were made among available models and desirable features were identified. Holistic scoring was chosen as the primary method of scoring. The *Math Advantage* Performance assessments offer the following features:

- **They model good instruction**
  The assessments are like mini lessons.

- **They are diagnostic.**
  By reviewing students' notes, teachers gain valuable insight into the thinking strategies that students are using.

- **They encourage the thinking process.**
  The assessments guide students through the process of organizing their thoughts and revising their strategies as they solve problems.

- **They are flexible.**
  No strict time limits are imposed,and students are encourage to proceed at their own pace.

- **They use authentic instruction.**
  Each task is based on realistic problem-solving situations.

- **They are scored holistically.**
  Each student's responses are scored holistically to provide a comprehensive view of his or her performance.

## Development of the Performance Assessment Program

Each assessment was field-tested with students before it was selected for inclusion in the program. After the assessments were selected, the pool of student papers for each assessment was reviewed and model papers were selected to illustrate the various scores. Annotations were then written for each model paper, explaining why the score was given.

The development process provided an opportunity to drop or correct those assessments that were not working as expected.

# Administering the Performance Assessments

- **Be encouraging.**
  Your role in administering the assessments should be that of a coach, motivating, guiding, and encouraging students to produce their best work.

- **Be clear.**
  The directions for the assessments are not standardized. If necessary, you may rephrase them for students.

- **Be supportive.**
  You may assist students who need help. The amount of assistance needed will vary depending on the needs and abilities of your students.

- **Be fair.**
  Allow students adequate time to do their best work. They should not feel that they could have done better if they had been given enough time.

- **Be flexible.**
  All students need not proceed through the assessments at the same rate and in the same manner.

- **Be involving.**
  Whenever possible, involve students in the evaluation process.

# Providing for Students with Special Needs

Many school districts are facing the challenge of adapting instruction and assessment to make them appropriate for their learners with special needs. Because the performance assessments are not standardized, the procedure for administering them can be adjusted to meet the needs of these learners. Teachers can help students who have difficulty responding by

- pairing a less proficient learner with a more proficient learner.

- encouraging students to discuss their ideas with a partner.

- providing an audiotape of the performance assessment and having students read along with the narration.

- permitting students to record tapes their response in lieu of a writing them.

- allowing students to do their initial planning, computing, designing, and drafting on the computer.

- giving students extra time to do their planning.

- providing assistance upon request.

Keep in mind, however, that the more the performance assessments are modified, the less reliable they may be as measures of students' mathematical ability.

# Scoring Rubrics for Mathematics

In scoring a student's task, the teacher should ask two questions: *How well did the student use the conventions of mathematics to arrive at a solution?* and *How well did the student communicate the solution* The scoring system used for the performance assessments is designed to be compatible with those used by many state assessment programs. Using a 4-point scale, the teacher classifies the student's performance as "excellent," "adequate," "limited," or "little or no achievement". A Score 3 paper shows evidence of extensive understanding of content and provides an exceptionally clear and effective solution. A Score 2 paper shows an acceptable understanding of content and provides a solution that shows reasonable insight. A Score 1 paper shows partial understanding and is clear in some parts, but not in others. A Score 0 paper demonstrates poor understanding of content and provides a solution that is unclear.

| 4-Point Scale | | | |
|---|---|---|---|
| Excellent Achievement | Adequate Achievement | Limited Achievement | Little or No Achievement |
| 3 | 2 | 1 | 0 |

# Sharing Results with Students and Parents

The performance assessment can provide valuable insights into students' mathematical abilities by revealing how all students performed on a common task. However, it is important that their performance on the assessment be interpreted in light of other samples that have been collected such as daily papers, student portfolios, and other types of tests, as well as teacher observation.

## For Students

Discuss the rubric with students and explain how it is used. You may even want to score some anonymous papers as a group or have students score each other's papers and discuss the criteria as they apply to those papers. Make photocopies of the rubrics to use for individual reports. Discuss the reports in conferences with students, pointing out their strengths as well as areas in which they could still improve.

## For Parents

Results of performance assessments may also be shared with parents, who will. appreciate seeing what their children can do. Show parents the performance assessment so that they understand the task that the students were asked to perform. Show their child's responses and discuss the strengths and weaknesses of the responses. Explain the scoring rubric and how the responses were evaluated. Show parents model papers that illustrate the range in student performance to help them put their child's paper in perspective.

## Using Results to Assign Grades

No single test, whether a standardized achievement test, a performance assessment, or an open-ended test, can fully measure a student's mathematical ability. For this reason it is important to use multiple measures of assessment. Therefore, a score on performance assessment should not be used as the sole determiner of a report-card grade or semester grade. The performance assessment could represent one of several factors used to determine a student's grade. Assessments could be combined with the results of a selection of tests, daily grades, class participation, self-reflections, and various samples collected in a portfolio. The following table shows how holistic scores can be converted into numerical or letter grades.

| Holistic Score | Letter Grade | Numerical Grade |
|---|---|---|
| 3 | A | 90-100 |
| 2 | B | 80-89 |
| 1 | C | 70-79 |
| 0 | D-F | 60 or below |

## Developing Your Own Rubric

A well-written rubric can help teachers score students' work more accurately and fairly. It also gives students a better idea of what qualities their work should exhibit. Using performance assessment to make connections between teaching and learning requires both conceptual and reflective involvement. Determining criteria may be the most difficult aspect of the process of developing assessment criteria on which to evaluate students' performance. Particularly challenging is the task of finding the right language to describe the qualities of student performance that distinguishes mediocre and excellent work. Teachers should begin the process of developing rubrics by

- gathering sample rubrics as models to be adapted as needed.

- selecting samples of students' work that represent a range of quality.

- determining the qualities of work that distinguish good examples from poor examples.

- using those qualities to write descriptors for the desired characteristics.

- continually revising the criteria until the rubric score reflects the quality of work indicated.

# *Your Own* **Scoring Rubric**

| Response Level | Criteria |
|---|---|
| **Score 3** | **Generally accurate, complete, and clear** <br><br> _____ <br><br> _____ <br><br> _____ <br><br> _____ |
| **Score 2** | **Partially accurate, complete, and clear** <br><br> _____ <br><br> _____ <br><br> _____ <br><br> _____ |
| **Score 1** | **Minimally accurate, complete, and clear** <br><br> _____ <br><br> _____ <br><br> _____ <br><br> _____ |
| **Score 0** | **Not accurate, complete, and clear** <br><br> _____ <br><br> _____ <br><br> _____ <br><br> _____ |

# Math Advantage Scoring Rubric

| Response Level | Criteria |
|---|---|
| **Score 3** | **Generally accurate, complete, and clear**<br><br>_____ All or most parts of the task are successfully completed; the intents of all parts of the task are addressed with appropriate strategies and procedures.<br><br>_____ There is evidence that the student has a clear understanding of key concepts and procedures.<br><br>_____ Student work and explanations are clear.<br><br>_____ Additional illustrations or information, if present, enhance communication.<br><br>_____ Answers for all parts are correct or reasonable. |
| **Score 2** | **Partially accurate, complete, and clear**<br><br>_____ Some parts of the task are successfully completed; other parts are attempted and their intents addressed, but they are not successfully completed.<br><br>_____ There is evidence that the student has partial understanding of key concepts and procedures.<br><br>_____ Some student work and explanations are clear, but it is necessary to make inferences to understand the response.<br><br>_____ Additional illustrations or information, if present, may not enhance communication significantly.<br><br>_____ Answers for some parts are correct, but partially correct or incorrect for others. |
| **Score 1** | **Minimally accurate, complete, and clear**<br><br>_____ A part (or parts) of the task is (are) addressed with minimal success while other parts are omitted or incorrect.<br><br>_____ There is minimal or limited evidence that the student understands concepts and procedures.<br><br>_____ Student work and explanations may be difficult to follow, and it is necessary to fill in the gaps to understand the response.<br><br>_____ Additional illustrations or information, if present, do not enhance communication and may be irrelevant.<br><br>_____ Answers to most parts are incorrect. |
| **Score 0** | **Not accurate, complete, and clear**<br><br>_____ No part of the task is completed with any success.<br><br>_____ There is little, if any, evidence that the student understands key concepts and procedures.<br><br>_____ Student work and explanations are very difficult to follow and may be incomprehensible.<br><br>_____ Any additional illustrations, if present, do not enhance communication and are irrelevant.<br><br>_____ Answers to all parts are incorrect. |

# PERFORMANCE ASSESSMENT

# Bubble Gum

## Purpose
To assess student performance after completing Chapters 1–9.

## Materials
compass, protractor

## Time
15 to 20 minutes per task

## Grouping
Individuals or partners

## Overview
Explain to students that this performance assessment is about bubble gum. Each task is about a situation related to the packaging, favorite flavors, or costs of bubble gum.

### Task A-1  Stacks of Packs!
Students are asked to find the amount of plastic needed to wrap 10 million packs of gum in sets of 20 packs and in sets of 25 packs and to express these values in scientific notation.

### Task A-2  Favorite Flavors
Students are asked to make a table and a graph to show the results of a survey on the favorite flavor of gum. Then they are asked to order the results from favorite flavor of the greatest number of students to favorite flavor of the least number of students and to interpret the results of the sample.

### Task A-3  Which Is the Better Buy?
Students are asked to determine the better buy based on the price and the number of pieces of gum in two packs. Then they are asked to find how many packs of the least expensive bubble gum they would need to buy to save a dollar. Finally, they are asked to consider the better buy, based on the number of grams each package weighs.

### Task A-4  Bulky Bubble Gum
Students are asked to find the price per piece for gum bought in bulk and what a distributor would have to pay for 150,000 pieces of gum. Then they determine how many pieces of each color the distributor would receive.

# Bubble Gum

| Task | Performance Indicators | Observations and Rubric Score (One score per task) |
|---|---|---|
| A-1 | _____ Determines the amount of plastic the manufacturer will need to wrap 10 million packs of gum in stacks of 20 packs. <br><br> _____ Expresses the answer in scientific notation. <br><br> _____ Determines the amount of plastic the manufacturer will need to wrap 10 million packs of gum in stacks of 25 packs. <br><br> _____ Expresses the answer in scientific notation. <br><br> _____ Subtracts to find the difference in the amounts of plastic needed to wrap the stacks of gum in the two different ways. <br><br> _____ Explains how the solutions were found. | 3   2   1   0 |
| A-2 | _____ Makes a table to show the results of the survey. <br><br> _____ Chooses an appropriate graph to show the results of the survey. <br><br> _____ Makes the graph, including a title, labels, and scales. <br><br> _____ Orders the results of the survey. <br><br> _____ Interprets the results for the sample. | 3   2   1   0 |
| A-3 | _____ Finds the unit price of the gum in each pack. <br><br> _____ Identifies the 15-pack as the better buy. <br><br> _____ Determines the number of packs of the least expensive gum you need to buy to save a dollar. <br><br> _____ Determines the weight of a stick of gum in each pack. <br><br> _____ Explains why the 5-piece pack is the better buy when the weight is considered. | 3   2   1   0 |
| A-4 | _____ Finds the price per piece for gum bought in bulk. <br><br> _____ Finds the number of bags of 12 dozen pieces needed to make 150,000 pieces of gum. <br><br> _____ Multiplies the number of bags needed by $3.99 to find the cost of 150,000 pieces of gum. <br><br> _____ Determines the number of pieces of each color gum received if 144,000 pieces were purchased. <br><br> _____ Explains the solution. | 3   2   1   0 |
| | | **Total Score** _____ /12 |

# Stacks of Packs!

A gum manufacturer packages gum for shipping by putting the individual packs of gum in stacks and wrapping the stacks with plastic.

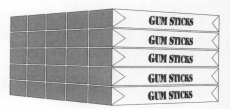

**a.** A manufacturer uses 0.0222 m² of plastic to wrap 20 packs of gum. How much plastic will the manufacturer need for wrapping 10 million packs of gum? Express your answer in scientific notation. Show and label your work. Explain your solution.

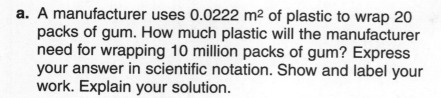

_____

_____

_____

**b.** The manufacturer decides that it will take less time to wrap 25 packs together instead of 20 packs. It takes 0.0291 m² to wrap 25 packs. How much plastic will the manufacturer need to wrap 10 million packs in groups of 25? Express your answer in scientific notation. Show and label your work. Explain your solution.

_____

_____

_____

_____

**c.** What is the difference in the amounts of plastic needed to wrap the stacks of gum in the two different ways? Show and label your work. Explain your solution.

_____

_____

_____

_____

_____

# Favorite Flavors

A sample of 6,000 middle school students in a community was asked, "What is your favorite flavor of gum?" The survey found that:

Favorite Gum Flavor

- $\frac{11}{30}$ of the sample chose grape

- $\frac{1}{12}$ of the sample chose strawberry

- $\frac{17}{60}$ of the sample chose Tootie Fruity

- $\frac{1}{15}$ of the sample chose watermelon

- $\frac{1}{5}$ of the sample chose cherry

**a.** Make a table and graph to show the survey results. Make sure that you show the percents and numbers of students who chose each flavor. Round to the nearest whole percent.

**b.** Put the results in order from favorite flavor of the greatest number of students to favorite flavor of the least number of students. Interpret the results for this sample. Use the data to support your interpretation.

*Show and label your work. Explain your solution for each part.*

_____

_____

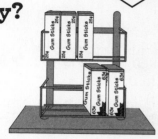

# Which is the better buy?

One pack of bubble gum with five pieces costs $0.25.
Another pack of bubble gum with 15 pieces costs $0.63.

**a.** Which pack is the better buy? Show and label your
work. Explain your solution.

_____
_____
_____
_____
_____

**b.** How many packs of the least expensive bubble gum would you need to
buy to save a dollar? Show and label your work. Explain your solution.

_____
_____
_____

**c.** The actual bubble gum (excluding the wrappers) in the 5-piece pack
weighs 24 g. The actual gum in the 15-piece pack of gum weighs 60 g.
Given this new information, do you still think the pack you chose in
part *a* is the better buy? Why or why not? Show and label your work.
Explain your solution.

_____
_____
_____
_____
_____
_____

# Bulky Bubble Gum!

You go to a wholesale warehouse and purchase a bag of bubble gum in bulk. The bag contains 12 dozen pieces and costs $3.99.

**a.** What is the cost per piece if you buy the gum in bulk?

⎯⎯⎯⎯⎯⎯⎯⎯⎯⎯⎯⎯⎯⎯⎯⎯⎯⎯⎯

⎯⎯⎯⎯⎯⎯⎯⎯⎯⎯⎯⎯⎯⎯⎯⎯⎯⎯⎯

**b.** A distributor needs 150,000 pieces on hand. How many bags of bubble gum would the distributor need to buy from the wholesale warehouse to get this amount? How much will the distributor have to pay for the gum?

⎯⎯⎯⎯⎯⎯⎯⎯⎯⎯⎯⎯⎯⎯⎯⎯⎯⎯⎯

⎯⎯⎯⎯⎯⎯⎯⎯⎯⎯⎯⎯⎯⎯⎯⎯⎯⎯⎯

⎯⎯⎯⎯⎯⎯⎯⎯⎯⎯⎯⎯⎯⎯⎯⎯⎯⎯⎯

**c.** The distributor decides to buy just 144,000 pieces in bulk and wants to figure out the number of pieces of each flavor. What is the number of pieces of each flavor? Show the distributor how you got your numbers if the following is true for each bag.

Each bag contains:

- 72 pieces of grape
- 36 pieces of strawberry
- 18 pieces of Tootie Fruity
- 9 pieces of watermelon
- 9 pieces of cherry

*Show and label your work. Explain your solution for each part.*

## Favorite Flavors

Name _____

Favorite Gum Flavor

A sample of 6,000 middle school students in a community was asked, "What is your favorite flavor of gum?" The survey found that:

- $\frac{11}{30}$ of the sample chose grape
- $\frac{1}{12}$ of the sample chose strawberry
- $\frac{17}{60}$ of the sample chose Tootie Fruity
- $\frac{1}{15}$ of the sample chose watermelon
- $\frac{1}{5}$ of the sample chose cherry

**a.** Make a table and graph to show the survey results. Make sure that you show the percents and numbers of students who chose each flavor. Round to the nearest whole percent.
Possible answers:

| Flavors | Percent | Number of Students |
| --- | --- | --- |
| grape | 37% | 2,200 |
| strawberry | 8% | 500 |
| Tootie Fruity | 28% | 1,700 |
| watermelon | 7% | 400 |
| cherry | 20% | 1,200 |

Favorite Gum Flavors of 6,000 Students

(pie chart: cherry, grape, strawberry, Tootie Fruity, watermelon)

**b.** Put the results in order from favorite flavor of the greatest number of students to favorite flavor of the least number of students. Interpret the results for this sample. Use the data to support your interpretation.

*Show and label your work. Explain your solution for each part.*

| Flavors | Percent | Number of Students |
| --- | --- | --- |
| grape | 37% | 2,200 |
| strawberry | 28% | 1,700 |
| Tootie Fruity | 20% | 1,200 |
| watermelon | 8% | 500 |
| cherry | 7% | 400 |

Possible answer: More than half the students surveyed liked grape or Tootie Fruity gum.

---

## Stacks of Packs!

Name _____

A gum manufacturer packages gum for shipping by putting the individual packs of gum in stacks and wrapping the stacks with plastic.

**a.** A manufacturer uses 0.0222 m² of plastic to wrap 20 packs of gum. How much plastic will the manufacturer need for wrapping 10 million packs of gum? Express your answer in scientific notation. Show and label your work. Explain your solution.

Possible answer: 10,000,000 ÷ 20 = 500,000

500,000 × 0.0222 = 11,100 m², or $1.11 \times 10^4$

Check students' explanations.

**b.** The manufacturer decides that it will take less time to wrap 25 packs together instead of 20 packs. It takes 0.0291 m² to wrap 25 packs. How much plastic will the manufacturer need to wrap 10 million packs in groups of 25? Express your answer in scientific notation. Show and label your solution.

Possible answer: 10,000,000 ÷ 25 =

400,000 packs

400,000 × 0.0291 = 11,640 m², or $1.164 \times 10^4$

Check students' explanations.

**c.** What is the difference in the amounts of plastic needed to wrap the stacks of gum in the two different ways? Show and label your work. Explain your solution.

11,640 m² − 11,100 m² = 540 m²; A manufacturer uses 540 m² more plastic to wrap 10 million packages of gum in packs of 25 than in packs of 20.

Check students' explanations.

## Bulky Bubble Gum!

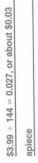

Name _____

You go to a wholesale warehouse and purchase a bag of bubble gum in bulk. The bag contains 12 dozen pieces and costs $3.99.

**a.** What is the cost per piece if you buy the gum in bulk?

$3.99 ÷ 144 = 0.027, or about $0.03
apiece

**b.** A distributor needs 150,000 pieces on hand. How many bags of bubble gum would the distributor need to buy from the wholesale warehouse to get this amount? How much will the distributor have to pay for the gum?

150,000 ÷ 144 = 1,041.66 bags,

or 1,042 bags

1,042 × $3.99 = $4,157.58

**c.** The distributor decides to buy just 144,000 pieces in bulk and wants to figure out the number of pieces of each flavor. What is the number of pieces of each flavor? Show the distributor how you got your numbers if the following is true for each bag.

Each bag contains:
- 72 pieces of grape
- 36 pieces of strawberry
- 18 pieces of Tootie Fruity
- 9 pieces of watermelon
- 9 pieces of cherry

*Show and label your work. Explain your solution for each part.*

144,000 ÷ 144 = 1,000 bags
72 pieces of grape × 1,000 bags = 72,000 pieces
36 pieces of strawberry × 1,000 bags = 36,000 pieces
18 pieces of Tootie Fruity × 1,000 bags = 18,000 pieces
9 pieces of watermelon × 1,000 bags = 9,000 pieces
9 pieces of cherry × 1,000 bags = 9,000 pieces

Bubble Gum A–4

14

---

## Which is the better buy?

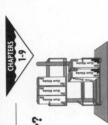

Name _____

One pack of bubble gum with five pieces costs $0.25. Another pack of bubble gum with 15 pieces costs $0.63.

**a.** Which pack is the better buy? Show and label your work. Explain your solution.

5-piece pack: $0.25 ÷ 5 = 0.05,

or $0.05 apiece

15-piece pack: $0.63 ÷ 15 = 0.042,

or $0.042 apiece

So, the 15 piece pack is a better buy.

**b.** How many packs of the least expensive bubble gum would you need to buy to save a dollar? Show and label your work. Explain your solution.

$0.05 − $0.042 = 0.008, You save $0.008 on each piece of

gum you buy, so you need to buy 143 pieces. 143 ÷ 15 = 9r8

So, you need to buy 10 packages of gum.

```
  9 r8
15)143
 −135
    8
```

**c.** The actual bubble gum (excluding the wrappers) in the 5-piece pack weighs 24 g. The actual gum in the 15-piece pack of gum weighs 60 g. Given this new information, do you still think the pack you chose in part a is the better buy? Why or why not? Show and label your work. Explain your solution.

In the 5-piece pack, each piece weighs 4.8 g and costs

$0.05. The cost per gram = $0.05 ÷ 4.8 g = 0.0104, or

$0.0104 per gram. In the 15-piece pack, each piece

weighs 4 g and costs $0.04. The cost per gram =

$0.042 ÷ 4 g = 0.0105, or $0.0105 per gram. Possible

answer: So, the 15-piece pack is not a better buy. You

get more grams per piece of gum in the 5-piece pack.

Bubble Gum A–3

13

---

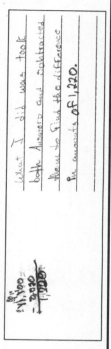

## Right paper (Level 2)

Name _____

### Stacks of Packs!

A gum manufacturer packages gum for shipping by putting the individual packs of gum in stacks and wrapping the stacks with plastic.

a. A manufacturer uses 0.0222 m² of plastic to wrap 20 packs of gum. How much plastic will the manufacturer need for wrapping 10 million packs of gum? Express your answer in scientific notation. Show and label your work. Explain your solution.

$$\frac{x}{10,000,000} = \frac{0.0222}{20}$$
$$x = 10,000,000 \cdot 0.0222 \div 20 = 11,000$$
$$1.11 \times 10^4$$

What I did was I made a proportion and got a Scientific Notation of 1.11×10⁴

b. The manufacturer decides that it will take less time to wrap 25 packs together instead of 20 packs. It takes 0.0291 m² to wrap 25 packs. How much plastic will the manufacturer need to wrap 10 million packs in groups of 25? Express your answer in scientific notation. Show and label your work. Explain your solution.

$$\frac{x}{10,000,000} = \frac{0.0291}{25}$$
$$x = 2.5$$
$$1.227 \times 10^4$$

What I did was I made a Proportion and got a Scientific Notation of 1.227×10⁴

c. What is the difference in the amounts of plastic needed to wrap the stacks of gum in the two different ways? Show and label your work. Explain your solution.

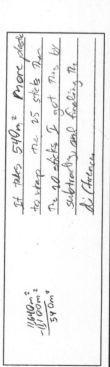

$$11,100$$
$$-\;\;2,020$$
$$\overline{\;\;1,000}$$

What I did was took both Answers out Subtracted them to find the difference in amounts of 1,220.

**Level 2** The student successfully used proportions to solve parts *a* and *b*, but did not have success in expressing the answers in scientific notation. The student appeared to understand the basic concepts of place value and measurement, but needs more experiences with scientific notation.

## Left paper (Level 3)

Name _____

### Stacks of Packs!

A gum manufacturer packages gum for shipping by putting the individual packs of gum in stacks and wrapping the stacks with plastic.

a. A manufacturer uses 0.0222 m² of plastic to wrap 20 packs of gum. How much plastic will the manufacturer need for wrapping 10 million packs of gum? Express your answer in scientific notation. Show and label your work. Explain your solution.

$$0.0222 \div 20 = 0.00111$$
$$0.00111 \cdot 10^7 = 11,100 \text{ m}^2$$

I first found out what it would take to wrap 1 package I then multiplied it by 10,000,000

b. The manufacturer decides that it will take less time to wrap 25 packs together instead of 20 packs. It takes 0.0291 m² to wrap 25 packs. How much plastic will the manufacturer need to wrap 10 million packs in groups of 25? Express your answer in scientific notation. Show and label your work. Explain your solution.

$$0.0291 \div 25 = 0.001164$$
$$0.001164 \cdot 10^7 = 11,640 \text{ m}^2$$

I did the same Thing above except I used 0.0291÷25 instead of 0.0222÷20.

c. What is the difference in the amounts of plastic needed to wrap the stacks of gum in the two different ways? Show and label your work. Explain your solution.

$$11,640 \text{ m}^2$$
$$-11,100 \text{ m}^2$$
$$\overline{\;\;\;540 \text{ m}^2}$$

It takes 540 m² more plastic to wrap me 25 sticks Ran The 20 sticks I got this by subtracting and finding the difference.

**Level 3** The student solved all parts of this task and demonstrated a clear understanding of the key concepts of measurement and place value. This was evidenced through answers to all three parts of the task. All responses were correct and there was work to support the answers.

# Model Student Papers for
# Bubble Gum

**TEACHER NOTES**

Name _____

## Stacks of Packs!

A gum manufacturer packages gum for shipping by putting the individual packs of gum in stacks and wrapping the stacks with plastic.

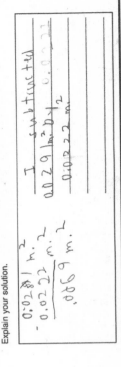

**a.** A manufacturer uses 0.0222 m² of plastic to wrap 20 packs of gum. How much plastic will the manufacturer need for wrapping 10 million packs of gum? Express your answer in scientific notation. Show and label your work. Explain your solution.

$$0.0222 \text{ m}^2$$
$$\times \ 10,000,000$$
$$\overline{222,000 \text{ m}^2}$$

I multiplied 0.0222 m² by 10 million

**b.** The manufacturer decides that it will take less time to wrap 25 packs together instead of 20 packs. It takes 0.0291 m² to wrap 25 packs. How much plastic will the manufacturer need to wrap 10 million packs in groups of 25? Express your answer in scientific notation. Show and label your work. Explain your solution.

$$0.0291 \text{ m}^2$$
$$\times \ 10,000,000$$
$$\overline{291,000 \text{ m}^2}$$

I multiplied 0.0291 m² by 10 million

**c.** What is the difference in the amounts of plastic needed to wrap the stacks of gum in the two different ways? Show and label your work. Explain your solution.

$$0.0291 \text{ m}^2$$
$$- \ 0.0222 \text{ m}^2$$
$$\overline{0.0069 \text{ m}^2}$$

I subtracted 0.0291 m² by 0.0222 m²

**Level 1** The student made a basic error in part *a* and did not recognize the relationship between the two stacks of gum. The student's work and explanations were clear but not correct. There was limited evidence that the student understands place value or scientific notation.

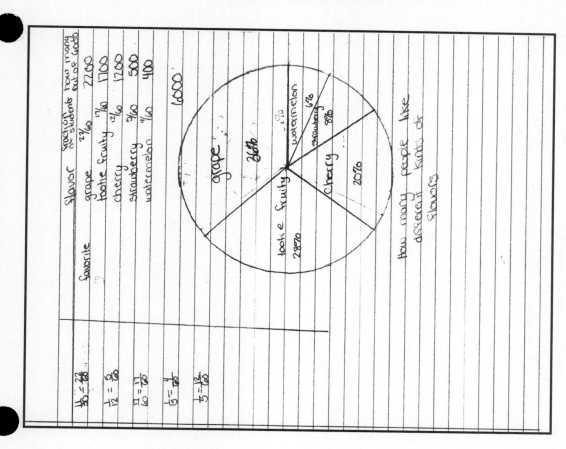

Favorite | Flavor | fraction of students | how many out of 6,000
--- | --- | --- | ---
| grape | 27/60 | 2200
| tootie fruity | 17/60 | 1700
| cherry | 12/60 | 1200
| strawberry | 3/60 | 500
| watermelon | 4/60 | 400
| | | 6,000

$\frac{11}{30} = \frac{22}{60}$

$\frac{1}{12} = \frac{5}{60}$

$\frac{17}{60} = \frac{17}{60}$

$\frac{1}{15} = \frac{4}{60}$

$\frac{1}{5} = \frac{12}{60}$

(Pie chart:)
grape 36%
tootie fruity 28%
cherry 8%
strawberry 6%
watermelon 6%
20%

How many people like different kinds of flavors

---

Name _____

A-2

CHAPTERS
1-9

## Favorite Flavors

A sample of 6,000 middle school students in a community was asked, "What is your favorite flavor of gum?" The survey found that:

- $\frac{11}{30}$ of the sample chose grape
- $\frac{1}{12}$ of the sample chose strawberry
- $\frac{17}{60}$ of the sample chose Tootie Fruity
- $\frac{1}{15}$ of the sample chose watermelon
- $\frac{1}{5}$ of the sample chose cherry

a. Make a table and graph to show the survey results. Make sure that you show the percents and numbers of students who chose each flavor. Round to the nearest whole percent.

(Favorite Gum Flavor)

b. Put the results in order from favorite flavor of the greatest number of students to favorite flavor of the least number of students. Interpret the results for this sample. Use the data to support your interpretation.

**Show and label your work. Explain your solution for each part.**

#1 grape 2200 1,3 more people like grape then tootie fruity.
#2 tootie fruity 1,700 14 more people like tootie fruity then cherry.
#3 cherry 1,200 24 more people like cherry then strawberry.
#4 strawberry 500 12 more people like strawberry then
watermelon.
#5 watermelon 400 5,5 more people like grape then
watermelon

First I changed all the fractions to 60 so
it would be easier to work with. Then I multiplied
the top and bottom by 100 so I would know how
many in 6,000, then I ranked them.

12

Bubble Gum A-2

## Level 3
The student demonstrated clear understanding of all key concepts. All the work was clear, complete, and accurate. The table and graph were accurate and well executed. All decision making is documented and explanations are clear.

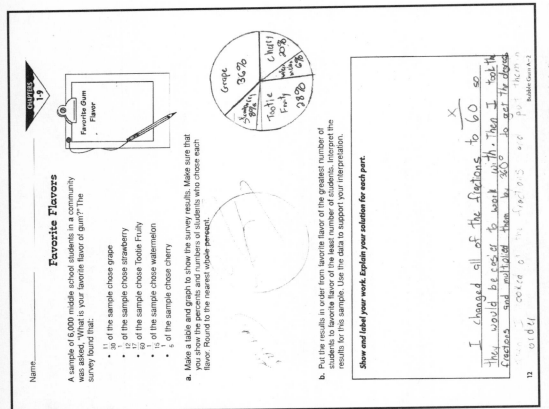

## Favorite Flavors

Name _____

A sample of 6,000 middle school students in a community was asked, "What is your favorite flavor of gum?" The survey found that:

- $\frac{11}{30}$ of the sample chose grape
- $\frac{1}{12}$ of the sample chose strawberry
- $\frac{17}{60}$ of the sample chose Tootie Fruity
- $\frac{1}{15}$ of the sample chose watermelon
- $\frac{1}{5}$ of the sample chose cherry

**a.** Make a table and graph to show the survey results. Make sure that you show the percents and numbers of students who chose each flavor. Round to the nearest whole percent.

**b.** Put the results in order from favorite flavor of the greatest number of students to favorite flavor of the least number of students. Interpret the results for this sample. Use the data to support your interpretation.

*Show and label your work. Explain your solution for each part.*

12

Bubble Gum A–2

**Level 2** The student's table was not well organized and did not include percents. The graph was correctly done and represented the data accurately. The student did not interpret the data as required in part *b* of the task.

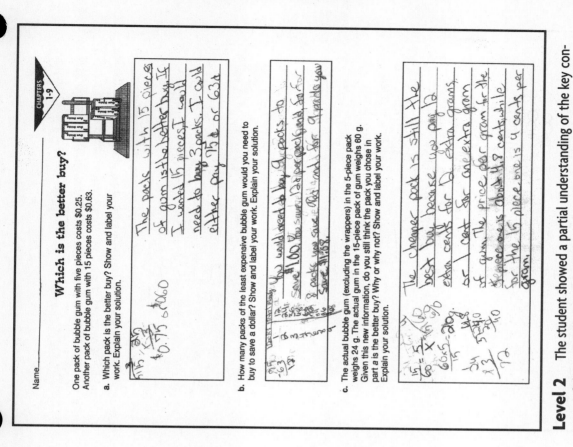

**Left paper (A-3):**

CHAPTERS
1-9

Name _____

### Which is the better buy?

One pack of bubble gum with five pieces costs $0.25.
Another pack of bubble gum with 15 pieces costs $0.63.

**a.** Which pack is the better buy? Show and label your work. Explain your solution.

5×4=15  4÷3
25×3=.75 for 15 pieces
with five pieces price.

15 pieces for 63¢ is the better
deal because 5×3=15 and 25×3=.75 for
15 pieces with 5 piece price and
with 15 piece pack it's only .63.

**b.** How many packs of the least expensive bubble gum would you need to buy to save a dollar? Show and label your work. Explain your solution.

.75-.63=.12 cont saved  You'd have to buy 9 packs to save
Packs money saved  a dollar because for every pack you save .12
1 .12  cents and 12×9=108
2 .24
3 .36
4 .48
5 .60

**c.** The actual bubble gum (excluding the wrappers) in the 5-piece pack weighs 24 g. The actual gum in the 15-piece pack of gum weighs 60 g. Given this new information, do you still think the pack you chose in part a is the better buy? Why or why not? Show and label your work. Explain your solution.

24×3=72g  No, because if you brought 3 5-piece
packs of gum for 25¢ you'd be getting
72g, but the one 15-piece pack of gum
is only get 60 g. That's 12g less!

7 | 84
8 | 96
9 | 108

Bubble Gum A-3                                                     13

**Right paper:**

CHAPTERS
1-9

Name _____

### Which is the better buy?

One pack of bubble gum with five pieces costs $0.25.
Another pack of bubble gum with 15 pieces costs $0.63.

**a.** Which pack is the better buy? Show and label your work. Explain your solution.

$1 ÷ .25
$0.75 = $0.60

The pack with 15 pieces
of gum is the better buy. If
I wanted 15 pieces I would
need to buy 3 packs. I could
either pay .75¢ or 63¢

**b.** How many packs of the least expensive bubble gum would you need to buy to save a dollar? Show and label your work. Explain your solution.

You would need to buy 9 packs to
save 1.00. You save 12¢ per pack and so for
8 packs you save .96¢ and for 9 packs you
save $1.08.

**c.** The actual bubble gum (excluding the wrappers) in the 5-piece pack weighs 24 g. The actual gum in the 15-piece pack of gum weighs 60 g. Given this new information, do you still think the pack you chose in part a is the better buy? Why or why not? Show and label your work. Explain your solution.

15 = 5 × X
60 = 5 × 89 = 90
60×5=300

The cheaper pack is still the
best buy because you pay 12
extra cents for 6 extra grams,
or 1 cent for one extra gram
of gum. The price per gram for the
15 piece is about 4.18 cents while
for the 15 piece one is 4 cents per
gram.

**Level 3** The student demonstrated an understanding of the key concepts of the tasks. The student identified the 15-pack as the better buy and determined the number of packs needed to save a dollar. The student attempted to explain why the 5-piece pack is the better buy.

**Level 2** The student showed a partial understanding of the key concepts of this task. The responses to parts *a* and *b* were correct and there was sufficient work to support the answers. The explanation in part *a* required the reader to make some inferences. The student did not succeed with part *c*.

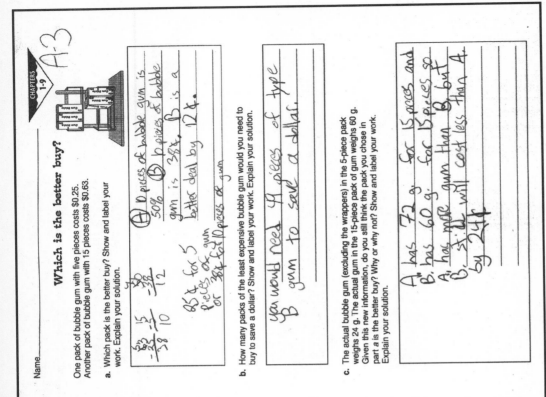

**Level 1** The student did not demonstrate understanding of the key concepts being assessed. In part *a* there was substitution of a % sign for the ¢ sign. The $.38 appeared without justification. There was no work to support the answer in parts *b* and *c*. There was minimal explanation.

**TEACHER NOTES**

## Level 3 paper (left)

Name _____

### Bulky Bubble Gum!

You go to a wholesale warehouse and purchase a bag of bubble gum in bulk. The bag contains 12 dozen pieces and costs $3.99.

a. What is the cost per piece if you buy the gum in bulk?

*12·12=144*
*144)$3.99*
The cost is $0.0277 per piece of gum

b. A distributor needs 150,000 pieces on hand. How many bags of bubble gum would the distributor need to buy from the wholesale warehouse to get this amount? How much will the distributor have to pay for the gum?

*1042 r66 =1042*
*144)150,000*
He will need 1042 bags
*1042·$3.99 = $4,157.58*
—for $4,157.58

c. The distributor decides to buy just 144,000 pieces in bulk and wants to figure out the number of pieces of each flavor. What is the number of pieces of each flavor? Show the distributor how you got your numbers if the following is true for each bag.

Each bag contains:
- 72 pieces of grape
- 36 pieces of strawberry
- 18 pieces of Tootie Fruity
- 9 pieces of watermelon
- 9 pieces of cherry

Show and label your work. Explain your solution for each part.

*144,000 ÷ 144 = 1000*
*72·1000 = 72,000 pieces of grape*
*36·1000 = 36,000 pieces of strawberry*
*18·1000 = 18,000 pieces of Tootie Fruity*
*9·1000 = 9,000 pieces of watermelon*
*9·1000 = 9,000 pieces of cherry*

I first found the number of packages and multiplied by each amount.

## Level 2 paper (right)

Name _____

### Bulky Bubble Gum!

You go to a wholesale warehouse and purchase a bag of bubble gum in bulk. The bag contains 12 dozen pieces and costs $3.99.

a. What is the cost per piece if you buy the gum in bulk?

*12·12=144*
*144)3.99*
*3.8¢*
the piece cost 2.8¢

b. A distributor needs 150,000 pieces on hand. How many bags of bubble gum would the distributor need to buy from the wholesale warehouse to get this amount? How much will the distributor have to pay for the gum?

*1042r6*
*144)150,000*
*1042*
*x 3.99*
he would need to by 1042 bags. cost $4,157.58.

c. The distributor decides to buy just 144,000 pieces in bulk and wants to figure out the number of pieces of each flavor. What is the number of pieces of each flavor? Show the distributor how you got your numbers if the following is true for each bag.

Each bag contains:
- 72 pieces of grape
- 36 pieces of strawberry
- 18 pieces of Tootie Fruity
- 9 pieces of watermelon
- 9 pieces of cherry

Show and label your work. Explain your solution for each part.

*1000*
*144)144,000*

14

## Level 2

The student has a correct solution for part *a* even though there could be more work to support the answer. In part *b*, a correct procedure is shown when the student multiplies the cost of one bag by 1,042 bags. Part *c* is accurate but there is little work to support the answer.

## Level 3

The student demonstrated clear understanding of the key concepts being addressed in this task. All responses were correct and there was sufficient work to support the answers. The explanation in part *c* was accurate and well documented.

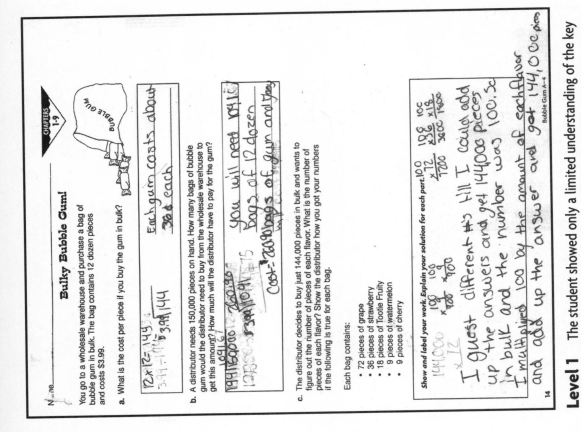

**Level 1** The student showed only a limited understanding of the key concepts being assessed in this task. In part *b*, the student used the correct number of bags of gum, but erroneously divided instead of multiplying to find the total price. In part *c*, the student made place-value errors.

**TEACHER NOTES**

# You Be the Teacher!

## Purpose
To assess student performance after completing Chapters 10–17.

## Materials
straightedge, cm ruler, pattern blocks

## Time
15 to 20 minutes per task

## Grouping
Individuals or partners

## Overview
Explain to students that this performance assessment is about being teachers. Each task is associated with techniques that could be used to teach younger students about a geometry concept or about patterns.

### Task B-1   A Teacher's Work Is Never Done
Students are asked to explain to fourth-grade students how to use marshmallows and straws to make prisms. They make a table to show the number of vertices and edges and then explain how they are related to the number of marshmallows and straws used.

### Task B-2   Coordinating Coordinates
Students are asked to explain to fifth-grade students about coordinates on a grid by showing them how to plot the ordered pairs for the coordinates of a six-sided polygon that is located in all four quadrants and has two pairs of sides parallel.

### Task B-3   Net Works
Students are asked to explain to younger students how to make two nets for regular hexagonal prisms. One net has edges that are half the length of the edges of the other net.

### Task B-4   Patterns and Trains
Students are asked to make a pattern that has a ratio of 3 triangles to 1 hexagon and a ratio of 2 triangles to 4 squares. Then they determine how many of each shape would be needed so that 20 students could make a train that is twice as long.

# You Be the Teacher!

| Task | Performance Indicators | Observations and Rubric Score (One score per task) |
|------|------------------------|----------------------------------------------------|
| B-1 | _____ Draws a diagram to illustrate vertices and edges on a prism.<br><br>_____ Makes a table to show the number of vertices and edges on rectangular, pentagonal, hexagonal, and octagonal prisms.<br><br>_____ Explains how many marshmallows and how many straws are needed to complete each prism. | 3   2   1   0 |
| B-2 | _____ Lists ordered pairs for the coordinates of a six-sided polygon that is not regular, is located in all four quadrants, and has two pairs of parallel sides.<br><br>_____ Plots the points on a grid.<br><br>_____ Changes the polygon so there is only one pair of parallel sides.<br><br>_____ Lists the ordered pairs for the coordinates of the new polygon.<br><br>_____ Explains the solutions. | 3   2   1   0 |
| B-3 | _____ Draws a net for a regular hexagonal prism.<br><br>_____ Draws a net for a second regular hexagonal prism with edges that are half the length of the first net. | 3   2   1   0 |
| B-4 | _____ Uses pattern blocks in the ratio 3 triangles to 1 hexagon and 2 triangles to 4 squares to make a train.<br><br>_____ Identifies the number of blocks of each shape in the train.<br><br>_____ Determines the number of pattern blocks in each of the three shapes that is needed so that 20 students can each make a train that is twice as long as the original train.<br><br>_____ Explains and labels the solution. | 3   2   1   0 |
| | **Total Score** _____ /12 | |

# A Teacher's Work is Never Done.

You have been asked to go into a fourth grade classroom to teach students how use marshmallows and straws to make the polyhedrons listed below.

- rectangular prism
- pentagonal prism
- hexagonal prism
- octagonal prism

**a.** You are making a worksheet for the student that explains how to build a prism. Your worksheet should describe a prism and give examples of a vertex and an edge. Draw a diagram to help explain these ideas to the fourth graders. Make a table so the fourth graders will know how many vertices and edges each prism has. Show and label your work. Explain your solution.

| | | |
|---|---|---|
| | | |
| | | |
| | | |
| | | |

**b.** How many marshmallows and straws will you need for each student to complete each polyhedron? Show and label your work. Explain your solution.

| | | |
|---|---|---|
| | | |
| | | |
| | | |

# Coordinating Coordinates

You will be teaching the fifth grade class about coordinates on a grid. You will check to see if they understand by having them graph a polygon on a grid.

**a.** To show them what to do, list the ordered pairs for the coordinates of a six-sided polygon that is not regular.

- Draw the polygon so that it is located in all four quadrants.
- Make two pairs of the sides of the polygon parallel.
- Label the vertices of the polygon.

Plot the points on a grid so that, when connected, you form a six-sided polygon that is not regular. Show and label your work. Explain your solution.

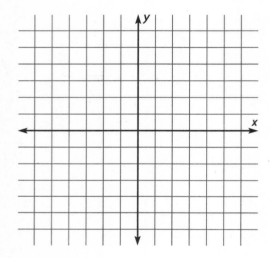

**b.** Change your polygon so there is only one pair of parallel sides. List the ordered pairs for the coordinates and plot the points on the grid to show the new polygon. Show and label your work. Explain your solution.

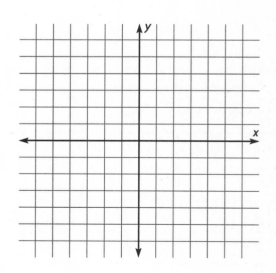

# Net Works

You will be teaching second-grade and fourth-grade students how to make a regular hexagonal prism from a net. The students use the net to make a hexagonal prism that can be used as a number cube for playing board games.

You need to draw a diagram of a pattern for the net. The pattern will be copied onto paper and given to each child. The children will fold the paper to make a hexagonal prism.

The size of the net for the fourth-grade class should be smaller than the net for the second-grade class. So, the edges of the fourth-grade nets should be half the size of the edges of the second-grade nets.

Draw the pattern for the nets for the second-grade and fourth-grade students. A pattern for the rectangular net is shown to help you get you started. Hint: You may want to modify this net for the hexagonal prism.

| | top | | |
|---|---|---|---|
| face 1 | face 2 | face 3 | face 4 |
| | bottom | | |

# Patterns and Trains

The third-grade class is studying patterns. You are going to assist them in completing a pattern for a freight train consisting of cattle cars (△), flat cars (○), and freight cars (□). Use pattern blocks to create a train that has a ratio of 3△ to 1○ and a ratio of 2△ to 4□.

⬡ flat car      △ cattle car      □ freight car

**a.** Make an answer key for the teacher that you could use to find the number of cars in a train. Show and label your work.

**b.** You will use blocks for the train cars. Build a train twice as long as the train in part *a*. How many blocks of each kind will you will need for each of 20 students to complete this activity? Show and label your work.

_____

_____

_____

_____

_____

---

CHAPTERS 10-17

Name _____

## Coordinating Coordinates

You will be teaching the fifth grade class about coordinates on a grid. You will check to see if they understand by having them graph a polygon on a grid.

**a.** To show them what to do, list the ordered pairs for the coordinates of a six-sided polygon that is not regular.

- Draw the polygon so that it is located in all four quadrants.
- Make two pairs of the sides of the polygon parallel.
- Label the vertices of the polygon.

Plot the points on a grid so that, when connected, you form a six-sided polygon that is not regular. Show and label your work. Explain your solution.

Possible grid:

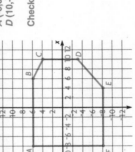

$A$ (-8,6), $B$ (6,6), $C$ (10,4), $D$ (10,-3), $E$ (4,-8), $F$ (-8,-8)

Check students' explanation.

**b.** Change your polygon so there is only one pair of parallel sides. List the ordered pairs for the coordinates and plot the points on the grid to show the new polygon. Show and label your work. Explain your solution.

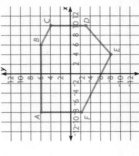

Possible answer: $A$ (-8,6), $B$ (6,6), $C$ (10,4), $D$ (10,-3), $E$ (4,-8), $F$ (-8,-2)

Check students' explanation.

28

---

CHAPTERS 10-17

Name _____

## A Teacher's Work is Never Done.

You have been asked to go into a fourth grade classroom to teach students how use marshmallows and straws to make the polyhedrons listed below.

- rectangular prism
- pentagonal prism
- hexagonal prism
- octagonal prism

**a.** You are making a worksheet for the student that explains how to build a prism. Your worksheet should describe a prism and give examples of a vertex and an edge. Draw a diagram to help explain these ideas to the fourth graders. Make a table so the fourth graders will know how many vertices and edges each prism has. Show and label your work. Explain your solution.

8 vertices

12 edges

| Prism | vertices | edges |
|---|---|---|
| rectangular prism | 8 | 12 |
| pentagonal prism | 10 | 15 |
| hexagonal prism | 12 | 18 |
| octagonal prism | 16 | 24 |

Possible answer: A rectangular prism has 8 vertices and 12 edges. The vertices are the points where the edges meet.

**b.** How many marshmallows and straws will you need for each student to complete each polyhedron? Show and label your work. Explain your solution.

| | Marshmallows | Straws |
|---|---|---|
| rectangular prism | 8 | 12 |
| pentagonal prism | 10 | 15 |
| hexagonal prism | 12 | 18 |
| octagonal prism | 16 | 24 |

27

---

Name _____

## Patterns and Trains

The third-grade class is studying patterns. You are going to assist them in completing a pattern for a freight train consisting of cattle cars (△), flat cars (○), and freight cars (□). Use pattern blocks to create a train that has a ratio of 3△ to 1○ and a ratio of 2△ to 4□.

○ flat car    △ cattle car    □ freight car

**a.** Make an answer key for the teacher that you could use to find the number of cars in a train. Show and label your work.

Possible answer: 1 train =

[pattern blocks row]

$$\triangle \quad \frac{6}{2} = \frac{3}{1}$$

$$\hexagon \quad \frac{6}{12} = \frac{1}{2}, \frac{2}{4} = \frac{1}{2}$$

Number of

△ = 6

⬡ = 2

□ = 12

**b.** You will use blocks for the train cars. Build a train twice as long as the train in part a. How many blocks of each kind will you will need for each of 20 students to complete this activity? Show and label your work.

2 ⬡ × 20 students = 40 ⬡ , 40 ⬡ × 2 trains = 80 ⬡

6 △ × 20 students = 120 △ , 120 △ × 2 trains = 240 △

12 □ × 20 students = 240 □ , 240 □ × 2 trains = 480 □

So, you will need 80 ⬡ , 240 △ , and 480 □ .

30

---

Name _____

## Net Works

You will be teaching second-grade and fourth-grade students how to make a regular hexagonal prism from a net. The students use the net to make a hexagonal prism that can be used as a number cube for playing board games.

You need to draw a diagram of a pattern for the net. The pattern will be copied onto paper and given to each child. The children will fold the paper to make a hexagonal prism.

The size of the net for the fourth-grade class should be smaller than the net for the second-grade class. So, the edges of the fourth-grade nets should be half the size of the edges of the second-grade nets.

Draw the pattern for the nets for the second-grade and fourth-grade students. A pattern for the rectangular net is shown to help you get you started. Hint: You may want to modify this net for the hexagonal prism.

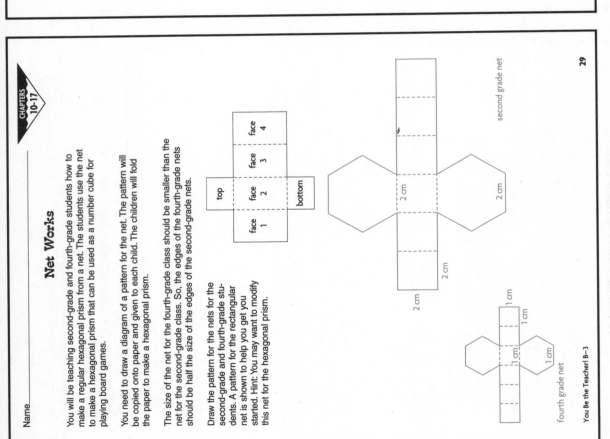

| top | face 2 | bottom |
| face 1 | face 3 | face 4 |

2 cm    2 cm    2 cm    2 cm

second grade net

1 cm    1 cm    1 cm    1 cm

fourth grade net

29

---

# Model Student Papers for
# You Be the Teacher!

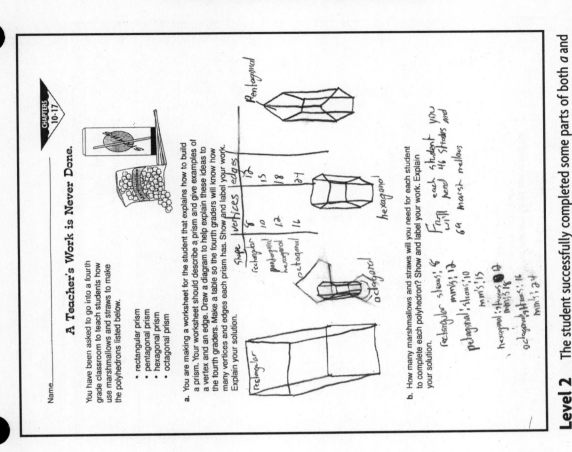

**Level 2** The student successfully completed some parts of both *a* and *b*. The drawings were correct but not labeled to show vertices and edges. The table showed the correct number of vertices and edges in the four polyhedrons. In part *b* the student demonstrated partial understanding of the concept.

**Level 3** The student demonstrated clear understanding of the key concepts being addressed in this task. All responses were correct and there was sufficient work to support the answers. The explanation in part *c* was accurate and well documented. The diagram indicated understanding of face, vertex, and edge.

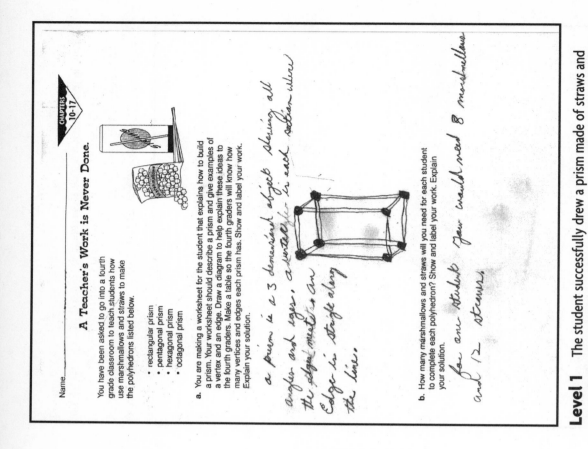

**CHAPTERS 10-17**

## A Teacher's Work is Never Done.

Name _____

You have been asked to go into a fourth grade classroom to teach students how to use marshmallows and straws to make the polyhedrons listed below.

- rectangular prism
- pentagonal prism
- hexagonal prism
- octagonal prism

**a.** You are making a worksheet for the student that explains how to build a prism. Your worksheet should describe a prism and give examples of a vertex and an edge. Draw a diagram to help explain these ideas to the fourth graders. Make a table so the fourth graders will know how many vertices and edges each prism has. Show and label your work. Explain your solution.

a prism is a 3 demensinal object shaving all angles and sges. a vertice is each ration where the edge meets. an edge is straight along the line.

**b.** How many marshmallows and straws will you need for each student to complete each polyhedron? Show and label your work. Explain your solution.

for one student you would need 8 marshmallows and 12 straws.

**TEACHER NOTES**

## Level 1

The student successfully drew a prism made of straws and marshmallows and gave an adequate explanation. There was no attempt to make a table with the number of vertices and edges for the four prisms. The student did not successfully complete part b.

---

**CHAPTERS 10-17**

Name _____

## Coordinating Coordinates

You will be teaching the fifth grade class about coordinates on a grid. You will check to see if they understand by having them graph a polygon on a grid.

a. To show them what to do, list the ordered pairs for the coordinates of a six-sided polygon that is not regular.

- Draw the polygon so that it is located in all four quadrants.
- Make two pairs of the sides of the polygon parallel.
- Label the vertices of the polygon.

Plot the points on a grid so that, when connected, you form a six-sided polygon that is not regular. Show and label your work. Explain your solution.

b. Change your polygon so there is only one pair of parallel sides. List the ordered pairs for the coordinates and plot the points on the grid to show the new polygon. Show and label your work. Explain your solution.

**Level 2** The student showed partial success in drawing polygons for the given conditions. The student was not able to correctly label all vertices with the ordered pairs for the coordinates in the two diagrams, and did not indicate two pairs of parallel sides for part *a* or any parallel sides for part *b*.

---

**CHAPTERS 10-17**

Name _____

## Coordinating Coordinates

You will be teaching the fifth grade class about coordinates on a grid. You will check to see if they understand by having them graph a polygon on a grid.

a. To show them what to do, list the ordered pairs for the coordinates of a six-sided polygon that is not regular.

- Draw the polygon so that it is located in all four quadrants.
- Make two pairs of the sides of the polygon parallel.
- Label the vertices of the polygon.

Plot the points on a grid so that, when connected, you form a six-sided polygon that is not regular. Show and label your work. Explain your solution.

There are 6 sides, and the line with vertices of (5,3) and (5,-2) is parallel with (-5,3) and (-5,-2). And the lines (-3,5) (3,5) and (-5,-2) (5,-2) are parallel

b. Change your polygon so there is only one pair of parallel sides. List the ordered pairs for the coordinates and plot the points on the grid to show the new polygon. Show and label your solution.

If again has 6 sides, but only (-3,5) (3,5) and (-5,-2) (5,-2) are parallel

**Level 3** The student demonstrated understanding of the key concepts assessed by this task. The student listed the coordinates asked for in the task accurately and drew diagrams that meet all required conditions. The work was accurate, complete, and clear.

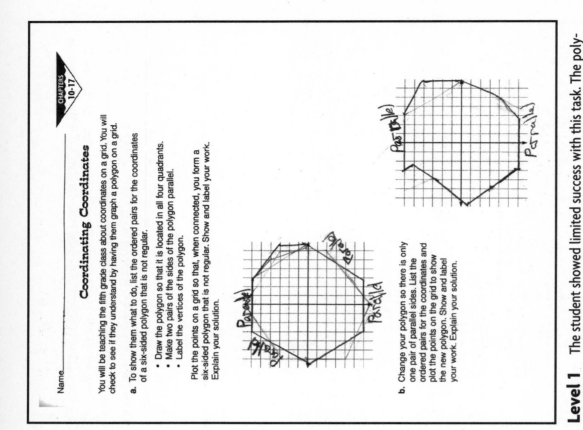

## Coordinating Coordinates

Name_____

You will be teaching the fifth grade class about coordinates on a grid. You will check to see if they understand by having them graph a polygon on a grid.

**a.** To show them what to do, list the ordered pairs for the coordinates of a six-sided polygon that is not regular.

- Draw the polygon so that it is located in all four quadrants.
- Make two pairs of the sides of the polygon parallel.
- Label the vertices of the polygon.

Plot the points on a grid so that, when connected, you form a six-sided polygon that is not regular. Show and label your work. Explain your solution.

**b.** Change your polygon so there is only one pair of parallel sides. List the ordered pairs for the coordinates and plot the points on the grid to show the new polygon. Show and label your work. Explain your solution.

**TEACHER NOTES**

**Level 1** The student showed limited success with this task. The polygon was not six-sided and the vertices were not labeled correctly. The student did not indicate any parallel sides for part *b*. There was no attempt to explain the solution.

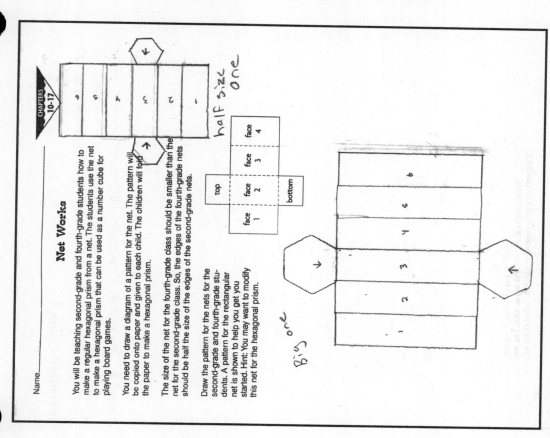

CHAPTERS 10-17

Name _____

### Net Works

You will be teaching second-grade and fourth-grade students how to make a regular hexagonal prism from a net. The students use the net to make a hexagonal prism that can be used as a number cube for playing board games.

You need to draw a diagram of a pattern for the net. The pattern will be copied onto paper and given to each child. The children will fold the paper to make a hexagonal prism.

The size of the net for the fourth-grade class should be smaller than the net for the second-grade class. So, the edges of the fourth-grade nets should be half the size of the edges of the second-grade nets.

Draw the pattern for the nets for the second-grade and fourth-grade students. A pattern for the rectangular net is shown to help you get you started. Hint: You may want to modify this net for the hexagonal prism.

**Level 2** The student demonstrated understanding of the key concepts assessed by this task. The student drew both diagrams successfully and labeled them clearly. However, the diagrams should have had the width and length of each panel in the larger net twice those of the smaller one.

---

CHAPTERS 10-17

Name _____

### Net Works

You will be teaching second-grade and fourth-grade students how to make a regular hexagonal prism from a net. The students use the nets to make a hexagonal prism that can be used as a number cube for playing board games.

You need to draw a diagram of a pattern for the net. The pattern will be copied onto paper and given to each child. The children will fold the paper to make a hexagonal prism.

The size of the net for the fourth-grade class should be smaller than the net for the second-grade class. So, the edges of the fourth-grade nets should be half the size of the edges of the second-grade nets.

Draw the pattern for the nets for the second-grade and fourth-grade students. A pattern for the rectangular net is shown to help you get you started. Hint: You may want to modify this net for the hexagonal prism.

**Level 3** The student demonstrated a clear understanding of the key concepts assessed by this task. The student drew both diagrams and labeled them clearly. The net for the fourth graders had edges that were about half the length of the edges of the net for the second graders.

**TEACHER NOTES**

Name _____

## Net Works

You will be teaching second-grade and fourth-grade students how to make a regular hexagonal prism from a net. The students use the net to make a hexagonal prism that can be used as a number cube for playing board games.

You need to draw a diagram of a pattern for the net. The pattern will be copied onto paper and given to each child. The children will fold the paper to make a hexagonal prism.

The size of the net for the fourth-grade class should be smaller than the net for the second-grade class. So, the edges of the fourth-grade nets should be half the size of the edges of the second-grade nets.

Draw the pattern for the nets for the second-grade and fourth-grade students. A pattern for the rectangular net is shown to help you get you started. Hint: You may want to modify this net for the hexagonal prism.

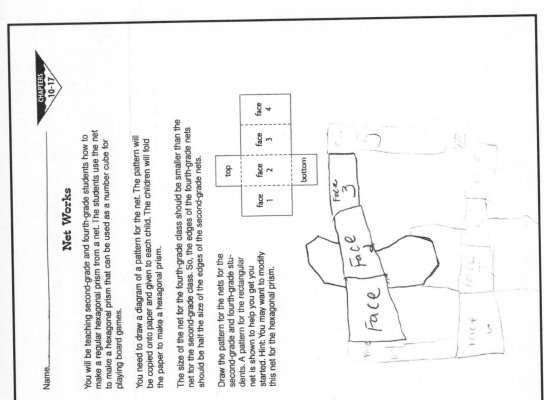

## Level 1
The student demonstrated minimal understanding of the key concepts assessed by this task. The diagram drawn did not adequately address the task and would not form any kind of polyhedron when cut and folded.

---

**Left paper:**

CHAPTERS
10-17

Name _____

## Patterns and Trains

The third-grade class is studying patterns. You are going to assist them in completing a pattern for a freight train consisting of cattle cars (△), flat cars (○), and freight cars (□). Use pattern blocks to create a train that has a ratio of 3△ to 1○ and a ratio of 2△ to 4□.

○ flat car   △ cattle car   □ freight car

**a.** Make an answer key for the teacher that you could use to find the number of cars in a train. Show and label your work.

There ar 3 triangles and 1 hexagon. Since 2△ to 4□ is the same as 1△ to 2□, I will have 6 squares.

**b.** You will use blocks for the train cars. Build a train twice as long as the train in part a. How many blocks of each kind will you need for each of 20 students to complete this activity? Show and label your work.

6 triangles x 20 = 120 △
2 hexagons x 20 = 40 ○
12 squares x 20 = 240 □   } needed for class of 20

You Be the Teacher! B–4

---

**Level 3**  The student demonstrated an understanding of the key concepts assessed by this task. The student had the correct ratios and was successful in drawing the train in part a. The student built the train in part b and described the number of blocks necessary for the students to build this train.

---

**Right paper:**

CHAPTERS
10-17

Name _____

## Patterns and Trains

The third-grade class is studying patterns. You are going to assist them in completing a pattern for a freight train consisting of cattle cars (△), flat cars (○), and freight cars (□). Use pattern blocks to create a train that has a ratio of 3△ to 1○ and a ratio of 2△ to 4□.

○ flat car   △ cattle car   □ freight car

**a.** Make an answer key for the teacher that you could use to find the number of cars in a train. Show and label your work.

6△ to 2○    6△ to 12□

△ = cattle car
○ = flat car
□ = freight car

**b.** You will use blocks for the train cars. Build a train twice as long as the train in part a. How many blocks of each kind will you need for each of 20 students to complete this activity? Show and label your work.

12△ to 6○    12△ 24□

I under stood the ratios, so I kept multiplying.

30

---

**Level 2**  The student demonstrated a partial understanding of the key concepts assessed by this task. The student had the ratios correct in part a and was successful in drawing the train. The student did not build the train in part b and did not find the correct number of blocks.

## Model Student Papers for
# You Be the Teacher!

CHAPTERS 10-17

Name________________________

CHAPTERS 10-17

6-4

**Patterns and Trains**

The third-grade class is studying patterns. You are going to assist them in completing a pattern for a freight train consisting of cattle cars (△), flat cars (○), and freight cars (□). Use pattern blocks to create a train that has a ratio of 3△ to 1○ and a ratio of 2△ to 4□.

⬡ flat car △ cattle car □ freight car

**a.** Make an answer key for the teacher that you could use to find the number of cars in a train. Show and label your work.

This works because I have 2 Δ for every 4□ and 3 Δ for every ⬠

**b.** You will use blocks for the train cars. Build a train twice as long as the train in part *a*. How many blocks of each kind will you will need for each of 20 students to complete this activity? Show and label your work.

10 X 20 = 200 Δ This is how many
16 X 20 = 320 □ I win need
2 X 20 = 40 ⬠

**Level 1** The student showed a limited understanding of the given ratios. The drawing in part *a* showed a ratio of 4 squares to 3 triangles. The student did not succeed in part *b*—no train was built, nor was the correct number of blocks needed for 20 students determined.

**TEACHER NOTES**

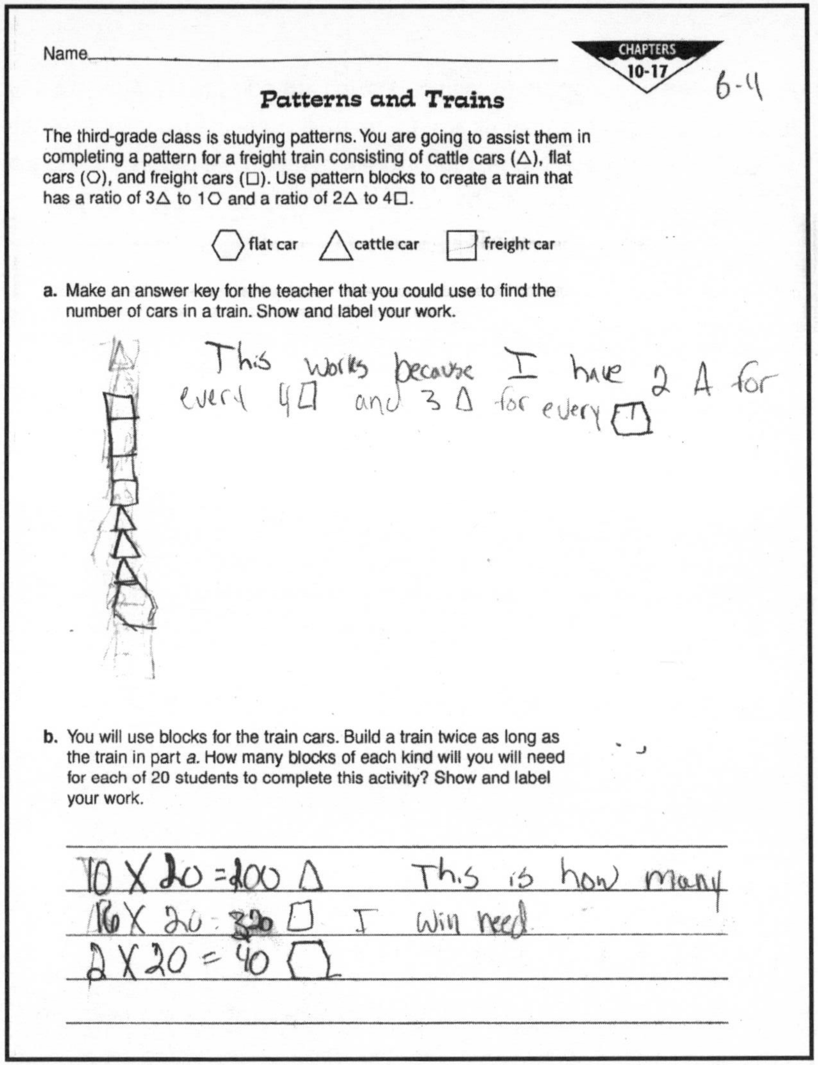

# Composting

## Purpose
To assess student performance after completing Chapters 18–23.

## Materials
cm ruler

## Time
15 to 20 minutes per task

## Grouping
Individuals or partners

## Overview
Explain to students that this performance assessment is about composting. Each task involves a situation about building a compost bin, materials in a compost heap, or worms or bacteria in a compost heap.

### Task C-1   Red Wiggler Farm
Students are asked to organize and graph data shown in a table about the number of worms counted in twenty samples of dirt. Then they find the measures of central tendency of the data and, based on the data collected, they estimate the number of worms that are in the whole tank of dirt.

### Task C-2   Compost Composite
Students are asked to determine the proper mix of materials containing carbon and nitrogen to make a compost heap. Then, based on the number of bins of each material, they find the probability that a randomly selected bin will contain a specific material.

### Task C-3   Building a Recycling Bin
Students are asked to make a scale drawing of a compost bin with four congruent rectangular faces. Then they find the volume in cubic feet of the bin.

### Task C-4   Bacteria Go to Work, Too!
Students are asked to make a table to show the growth pattern of one bacterium that doubles every 20 minutes. Then they write an algebraic expression to represent this number for any number of 20-min periods.

Name _____ Date _____

# Composting

| Task | Performance Indicators | Observations and Rubric Score (One score per task) |
|------|------------------------|-----------------------------------------|
| C-1 | _____ Organizes and displays the data about the number of worms counted by the students. <br><br> _____ Finds the mean for the data. <br><br> _____ Finds the median for the data. <br><br> _____ Finds the mode for the data. <br><br> _____ Explains what the measures of central tendency mean. <br><br> _____ Uses the data to estimate the number of worms in the whole tank. | 3  2  1  0 |
| C-2 | _____ Determines the amount of carbon in the organic materials. <br><br> _____ Determines the number of kilograms of nitrogen needed to get the proper mix of 25 parts carbon to 1 part nitrogen. <br><br> _____ Determines the probabilities that a randomly selected bin will contain each of the four possible materials. | 3  2  1  0 |
| C-3 | _____ Makes a diagram drawn to scale of the base of the bin. <br><br> _____ Makes a scale drawing of the compost bin. <br><br> _____ Finds the volume in cubic feet of the bin. <br><br> _____ Labels the diagrams. | 3  2  1  0 |
| C-4 | _____ Makes a table to show the pattern of growth. <br><br> _____ Writes an algebraic expression to represent the number of bacteria for any number of 20-min periods. <br><br> _____ Explains the solutions. | 3  2  1  0 |

Total Score _____/12

# Red Wiggler Farm

A seventh grade class has a worm farm with red wigglers in a 20-gal tank. The teacher needs to know about how many of these worms are in the farm. Twenty students in the class each take a 16-oz jar of dirt from the farm and count the worms in their jars. The numbers of worms counted by the students are:

| 2 | 3 | 2 | 4 | 5 |
|---|---|---|---|---|
| 5 | 6 | 1 | 4 | 4 |
| 2 | 1 | 5 | 1 | 2 |
| 4 | 2 | 3 | 3 | 1 |

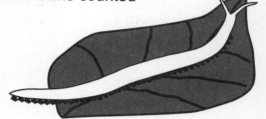

**a.** Organize and display the data the students collected. Find the measures of central tendency of the data. Show and label your work. Explain your solution.

| | |
|---|---|
| | |
| | |
| | |
| | |
| | |
| | |

_____

_____

_____

**b.** Using the data collected, determine how many worms you think are in the tank? Show and label your work. Explain your reasoning. (Hint: 1 gal = 128 oz)

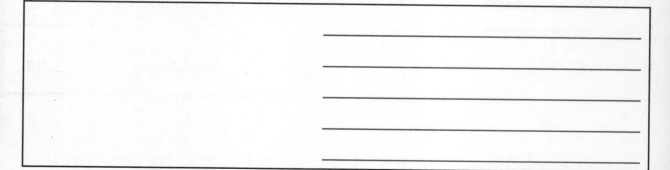

_____

_____

_____

_____

_____

# Compost Composite

You need the proper mix of materials containing carbon and nitrogen to make a compost heap. You have gathered these organic materials which contain 80% carbon.

- 75 kg grass clippings
- 23 kg oak leaves
- 34 kg vegetable trimmings
- 28 kg dead bean and pea plants

**a.** The compost heap requires a ratio of 25 parts carbon to 1 part nitrogen mixture. To get the proper mix, about how many kilograms of nitrogen do you need? Explain your solution.

**b.** Mother Earth Compost farm distributes organic materials to people who want to start their own compost heap. A new shipment contains:

- 4 bins with only grass clippings
- 7 bins with only oak leaves
- 6 bins with only vegetable trimmings
- 3 bins with only dead bean and pea plants

Gretchen is in the process of labeling the bins. She selects the bins at random. What is the probability that the first bin she labels contains grass clippings? oak leaves? vegetable trimmings? dead bean and pea plants?

# Building a Recycling Bin

Suppose you are going to build a recycling bin. The bin will have four congruent rectangular faces.

Each face will be rectangular in shape with dimensions of 3 ft in height and 4 ft in length.

Recyclable Paper

Recyclable Plastic

Recyclable Glass

**a.** You will build your bin on the top of a grassy area. Make a diagram that shows the shape and the dimensions of the base of your bin. Draw the dimensions to scale. Be sure to include your scale. Show and label your work.

**b.** Make a scale drawing of the compost bin. Find the volume in feet of your bin. Be sure to include your scale. Show and label your work.

# Bacteria Go to Work, Too!

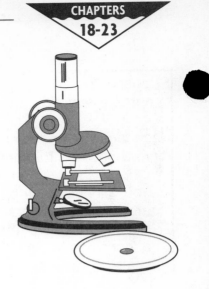

Your class is studying bacteria. You learn that one
bacterium doubles every 20 min and a drop of water
contains millions of bacteria.

**a.** Consider the growth pattern of one bacterium. If you start
with one bacterium, how many bacteria will there be at the
end of 4 hr? Make a table to display this growth. Show and
label your work. Explain your solution.

_____

_____

_____

_____

**b.** Find a pattern to help you calculate the number of bacteria in any
20-min period. Write an algebraic expression to represent this
number for any number of 20-min periods. Show and label your
work. Explain your solution.

_____

_____

_____

_____

_____

---

## Red Wiggler Farm

CHAPTERS 18-23

Name _____

A seventh grade class has a worm farm with red wigglers in a 20-gal tank. The teacher needs to know about how many of these worms are in the farm. Twenty students in the class each take a 16-oz jar of dirt from the farm and count the worms in their jars. The numbers of worms counted by the students are:

| 2 | 3 | 2 | 4 | 5 |
|---|---|---|---|---|
| 5 | 6 | 1 | 4 | 4 |
| 2 | 1 | 5 | 1 | 2 |
| 4 | 2 | 3 | 3 | 1 |

a. Organize and display the data the students collected. Find the measures of central tendency of the data. Show and label your work. Explain your solution. Check students graphs. Possible table:

| Number of Worms in the Jar | Frequency |
|---|---|
| 1 | 4 |
| 2 | 5 |
| 3 | 3 |
| 4 | 4 |
| 5 | 3 |
| 6 | 1 |

Possible graph: Line Plot

```
                    X
        X   X       X
    X   X   X   X   X
    X   X   X   X   X   X
    +---+---+---+---+---+---+
    0   1   2   3   4   5   6
      Number of Worms in the Jar
```

Possible answer: median 3, mode 2, mean 3 worms. There are about 3 worms in a 16 oz jar.

b. Using the data collected, determine how many worms you think are in the tank? Show and label your work. Explain your reasoning. (Hint: 1 gal = 128 oz)

20 gal × 128 oz = 2,560 oz

2,560 oz ÷ 16 = 160 jars

160 jars × 3 worms = 480 worms;

So, there are about 480 worms in the 20-gal tank.

Composting C–1                                                                 43

---

## Compost Composite

CHAPTERS 18-23

Name _____

You need the proper mix of materials containing carbon and nitrogen to make a compost heap. You have gathered these organic materials which contain 80% carbon.

- 75 kg grass clippings
- 34 kg vegetable trimmings
- 23 kg oak leaves
- 28 kg dead bean and pea plants

a. The compost heap requires a ratio of 25 parts carbon to 1 part nitrogen mixture. To get the proper mix, about how many kilograms of nitrogen do you need? Explain your solution.

75 kg of grass clippings × 80% = 60 kg carbon

23 kg of oak leaves × 80% = 18.4 kg carbon

34 kg of vegetable trimmings × 80% = 27.2 kg carbon

28 kg of dead bean and pea plants × 80% = 128 kg carbon

22.4 kg carbon

60 kg + 18.4 kg + 27.2 kg + 22.4 kg = 128 kg

128 ÷ 25 = 5.12, So, you will need about 5 kg of nitrogen for the compost heap.

b. Mother Earth Compost farm distributes organic materials to people who want to start their own compost heap. A new shipment contains:

- 4 bins with only grass clippings
- 7 bins with only oak leaves
- 6 bins with only vegetable trimmings
- 3 bins with only dead bean and pea plants

Gretchen is in the process of labeling the bins. She selects the bins at random. What is the probability that the first bin she labels contains grass clippings? oak leaves? vegetable trimmings? dead bean and pea plants?

grass clippings: $\frac{4}{20}$, $\frac{1}{5}$, or 20%; oak leaves: $\frac{7}{20}$, or 35%; vegetable trimmings: $\frac{6}{20}$, $\frac{3}{5}$, or 30%; dead bean and pea plants: $\frac{3}{20}$, or 15%

Composting C–2                                                                 44

---

## Building a Recycling Bin

CHAPTERS 18-23

Name _____

Suppose you are going to build a recycling bin. The bin will have four congruent rectangular faces.

Each face will be rectangular in shape with dimensions of 3 ft in height and 4 ft in length.

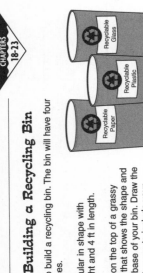

**a.** You will build your bin on the top of a grassy area. Make a diagram that shows the shape and the dimensions of the base of your bin. Draw the dimensions to scale. Be sure to include your scale. Show and label your work.

4 ft

4 ft

Scale: 1 cm = 1 ft

**b.** Make a scale drawing of the compost bin. Find the volume in feet of your bin. Be sure to include your scale. Show and label your work.

$V = 3 \text{ ft} \times 3 \text{ ft} \times 4 \text{ ft} = 36 \text{ ft}^2$

Scale:
1 cm = 1 ft

3 ft

4 ft

3 ft

4 ft

Composting C–3

45

## Bacteria Go to Work, Too!

CHAPTERS 18-23

Name _____

Your class is studying bacteria. You learn that one bacterium doubles every 20 min and a drop of water contains millions of bacteria.

**a.** Consider the growth pattern of one bacterium. If you start with one bacterium, how many bacteria will there be at the end of 4 hr? Make a table to display this growth. Show and label your work. Explain your solution.

| Bacteria Growth Rate | |
|---|---|
| 20-min Period (n) | Number of Bacteria |
| 1 | 1 |
| 2 | 2 |
| 3 | 4 |
| 4 | 8 |
| 5 | 16 |
| 6 | 32 |
| 7 | 64 |
| 8 | 128 |
| 9 | 256 |
| 10 | 512 |
| 11 | 1,024 |
| 12 | 2,048 |

Hour 1 — periods 1–3
Hour 2 — periods 4–6
Hour 3 — periods 7–9
Hour 4 — periods 10–12

Check students' explanations.

_____
_____
_____

**b.** Find a pattern to help you calculate the number of bacteria in any 20-min period. Write an algebraic expression to represent this number for any number of 20-min periods. Show and label your work. Explain your solution.

$2^{n-1}$, where $n$ = the number of 20-min periods

Check students' explanations.

_____
_____
_____

Composting C–4

46

---

Name _____

### Red Wiggler Farm

CHAPTERS 18-23

A seventh grade class has a worm farm with red wigglers in a 20-gal tank. The teacher needs to know about how many of these worms are in the farm. Twenty students in the class each take a 16-oz jar of dirt from the farm and count the worms in their jars. The numbers of worms counted by the students are:

| 2 | 3 | 2 | 4 | 5 |
|---|---|---|---|---|
| 5 | 6 | 1 | 4 | 4 |
| 2 | 1 | 5 | 1 | 2 |
| 4 | 2 | 3 | 3 | 1 |

a. Organize and display the data the students collected. Find the measures of central tendency of the data. Show and label your work. Explain your solution.

2+3+2+4+5+5+6+1+4+4+2+1+5+1+2+4+2+3+3+1

$$20\overline{)60}$$
$$\begin{array}{r}3 \\ +60 \\ \hline 00\end{array}$$
3 per jar

Mode = 2
median = 3
Mean = 3
range = 5

added up all the numbers, got 60. 60÷20=3
then found mode, median, mean and range

b. Using the data collected, determine how many worms you think are in the tank? Show and label your work. Explain your reasoning.
(Hint: 1 gal = 128 oz)

$$\frac{3}{16} = \frac{x}{160}$$

1 × 160 = 160    3 × 160 = 480
x = 480

I set up a proportion
and 3 × 160 = 480

**Level 2** The student demonstrated a partial understanding of the key concepts and procedures assessed in the task. The student gave correct values for mean, median, and mode, but only gave sufficient work to support finding the mean.

---

Name _____

### Red Wiggler Farm

CHAPTERS 18-23

A seventh grade class has a worm farm with red wigglers in a 20-gal tank. The teacher needs to know about how many of these worms are in the farm. Twenty students in the class each take a 16-oz jar of dirt from the farm and count the worms in their jars. The numbers of worms counted by the students are:

| 2 | 3 | 2 | 4 | 5 |
|---|---|---|---|---|
| 5 | 6 | 1 | 4 | 4 |
| 2 | 1 | 5 | 1 | 2 |
| 4 | 2 | 3 | 3 | 1 |

a. Organize and display the data the students collected. Find the measures of central tendency of the data. Show and label your work. Explain your solution.

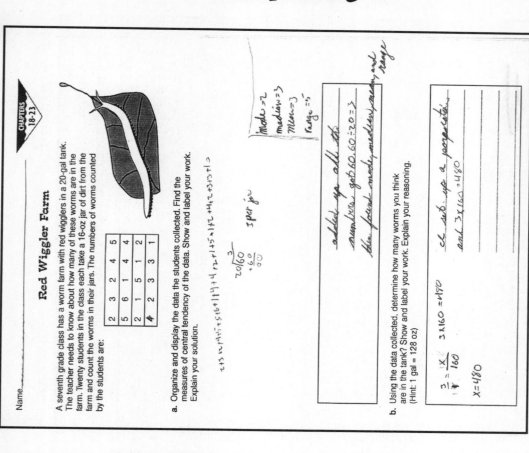

mean - ③
median - ③
mode - ②
range - ⑤

The mean is 3,
The median is 3,
The mode is 2,
and the range is 5.

I figured the measures of central tendency to be 3, 3, 2, and 5.

b. Using the data collected, determine how many worms you think are in the tank? Show and label your work. Explain your reasoning.
(Hint: 1 gal = 128 oz)

$$\frac{3}{16} = \frac{x}{128}$$

$$\frac{3 \cdot 128}{16} = \frac{384}{16} = 24 \text{ worms per gallon}$$

24 · 20 = 480 worms in the tank

I got 480 worms

I found out by finding the worms per gallon by proportion to find out how many worms are in 1 gallon and multiplied by 20.

**Level 3** The student demonstrated a clear understanding of the concepts and procedures assessed in the task. The data were organized well to show how the mean, median, and mode were found. All answers were correct.

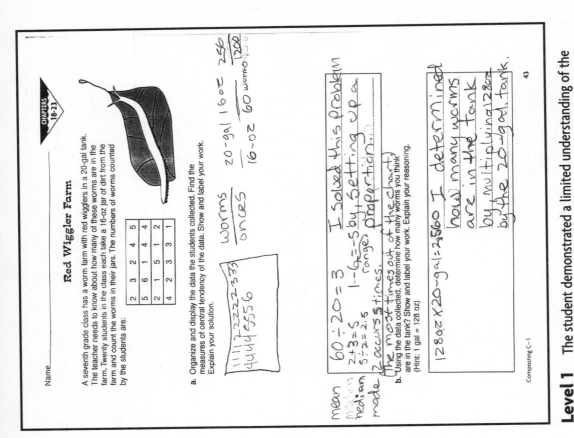

**CHAPTERS 18-23**

## Red Wiggler Farm

Name _____

A seventh grade class has a worm farm with red wigglers in a 20-gal tank. The teacher needs to know about how many of these worms are in the farm. Twenty students in the class each take a 16-oz jar of dirt from the farm and count the worms in their jars. The numbers of worms counted by the students are:

| 2 | 3 | 2 | 4 | 5 |
| 5 | 6 | 1 | 4 | |
| 2 | 1 | 5 | 1 | 2 |
| 4 | 2 | 3 | 3 | 1 |

a. Organize and display the data the students collected. Find the measures of central tendency of the data. Show and label your work. Explain your solution.

worms
ounces

1112222333
4445556

mean
median    60 ÷ 20 = 3    I solved this problem
median    2+3=5          1÷6=-5 by setting up a
          5÷2=2.5        range proportion.
mode    2 occurs 5 times.
        The most times out of the chart

b. Using the data collected, determine how many worms you think are in the tank? Show and label your work. Explain your reasoning.
(Hint: 1 gal = 128 oz)

20-gal 16oz  256
           ──────  128
16-oz      60 worms?

128oz × 20-gal = 2,560  I determined
                        how many worms
                        are in the tank
                        by multiplying 128oz
                        by the 20-gal tank.

Composting C-1    43

## Level 1

The student demonstrated a limited understanding of the concepts and procedures assessed in the task. The student gave correct values for mean and mode, but made an error in finding the median. The work was difficult to follow and included extraneous and incorrect numbers and computations.

**TEACHER NOTES**

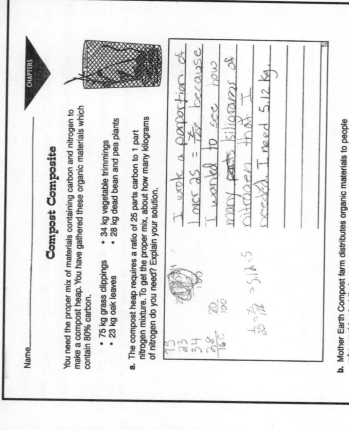

Name _____

### Compost Composite

You need the proper mix of materials containing carbon and nitrogen to make a compost heap. You have gathered these organic materials which contain 80% carbon.

- 75 kg grass clippings
- 23 kg oak leaves
- 34 kg vegetable trimmings
- 28 kg dead bean and pea plants

**a.** The compost heap requires a ratio of 25 parts carbon to 1 part nitrogen mixture. To get the proper mix, about how many kilograms of nitrogen do you need? Explain your solution.

*(handwritten student work)*
I wrote a proportion of 25/25 = x/x because I wanted to see how many parts kilograms of nitrogen that I needed. I need 5.12 kg.

**b.** Mother Earth Compost farm distributes organic materials to people who want to start their own compost heap. A new shipment contains:

- 4 bins with only grass clippings
- 7 bins with only oak leaves
- 6 bins with only vegetable trimmings
- 3 bins with only dead bean and pea plants

Gretchen is in the process of labeling the bins. She selects the bins at random. What is the probability that the first bin she labels contains grass clippings? oak leaves? vegetable trimmings? dead bean and pea plants?

*(handwritten student work)*
grass clippings - 4/20 = 1/5
oak leaves - 7/20
vegetable trimmings - 6/20 = 3/10
dead bean and pea plants - 3/20

grass clips - 1/5  40%
oak leaves - 7/20  10%
vegetable trimmings - 3/10  60%
dead pea + bean - 3/20  30%

**Level 2**  The student demonstrated a partial understanding of the concepts and procedures assessed in the task. The student correctly answered part *a*, but did not give sufficient support to show why 128 kg was used in the proportion. In part *b*, the probabilities are correct in fraction form.

---

Name _____

### Compost Composite

You need the proper mix of materials containing carbon and nitrogen to make a compost heap. You have gathered these organic materials which contain 80% carbon.

- 75 kg grass clippings
- 23 kg oak leaves
- 34 kg vegetable trimmings
- 28 kg dead bean and pea plants

**a.** The compost heap requires a ratio of 25 parts carbon to 1 part nitrogen mixture. To get the proper mix, about how many kilograms of nitrogen do you need? Explain your solution.

*(handwritten student work)*
You need about 5 kilograms of nitrogen. I knew this because I found 80% which is the carbon and then I set up a proportion to find out the kilograms of nitrogen.

160 ÷ ... = 5 kg

128 kg carbon

**b.** Mother Earth Compost farm distributes organic materials to people who want to start their own compost heap. A new shipment contains:

- 4 bins with only grass clippings
- 7 bins with only oak leaves
- 6 bins with only vegetable trimmings
- 3 bins with only dead bean and pea plants

Gretchen is in the process of labeling the bins. She selects the bins at random. What is the probability that the first bin she labels contains grass clippings? vegetable trimmings? dead bean and pea plants?

*(handwritten student work)*
I need to divide the number of bins of each one by the total number of bins which is 20.

grass clippings = 20% probability
oak leaves = 35% probability
vegetable trimmings = 30% probability
dead bean and pea plants = 15% probability

**Level 3**  The student demonstrated a clear and complete understanding of all the key concepts required to solve this task. The amounts of plant material were totaled and 80% of the total was found. The probability of selecting any of the bins was determined accurately and there was work to support the answers.

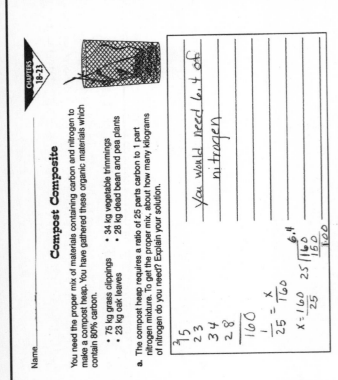

CHAPTERS 18-23

## Compost Composite

You need the proper mix of materials containing carbon and nitrogen to make a compost heap. You have gathered these organic materials which contain 80% carbon.

- 75 kg grass clippings
- 23 kg oak leaves
- 34 kg vegetable trimmings
- 28 kg dead bean and pea plants

**a.** The compost heap requires a ratio of 25 parts carbon to 1 part nitrogen mixture. To get the proper mix, about how many kilograms of nitrogen do you need? Explain your solution.

*You would need le.4 of nitrogen*

```
 75
 23
 34
 28
———
160
```

$$\frac{1}{25} = \frac{x}{160}$$

$$x = 160 \quad 25\overline{)160} \quad \frac{6.4}{160}$$
$$\frac{}{25} \qquad \frac{160}{100}$$

**b.** Mother Earth Compost farm distributes organic materials to people who want to start their own compost heap. A new shipment contains:

- 4 bins with only grass clippings
- 7 bins with only oak leaves
- 6 bins with only vegetable trimmings
- 3 bins with only dead bean and pea plants

Gretchen is in the process of labeling the bins. She selects the bins at random. What is the probability that the first bin she labels contains grass clippings? oak leaves? vegetable trimmings? dead bean and pea plants?

*I don't Know*

**TEACHER NOTES**

**Level 1** The student demonstrated minimal understanding of the key concepts and procedures required for solving this task. The student did not recognize that only 80% of the total amount of material is carbon. The student made no attempt to solve part *b* of the task.

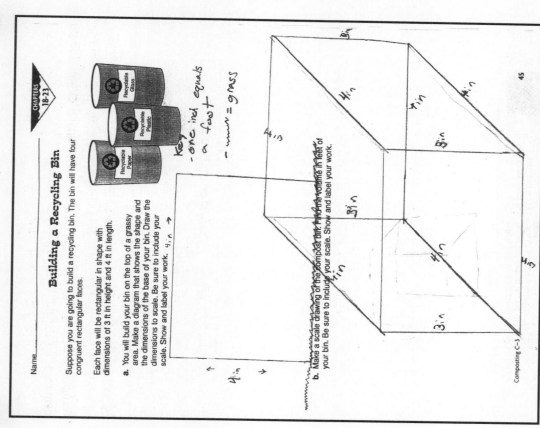

**Top paper (Level 2):**

CHAPTERS 18-23

Name _____

### Building a Recycling Bin

Suppose you are going to build a recycling bin. The bin will have four congruent rectangular faces.

Each face will be rectangular in shape with dimensions of 3 ft in height and 4 ft in length.

a. You will build your bin on the top of a grassy area. Make a diagram that shows the shape and the dimensions of the base of your bin. Draw the dimensions to scale. Be sure to include your scale. Show and label your work.

Key
- one inch equals a foot
= grass

b. Make a scale drawing of the compost bin. Find the volume in feet of your bin. Be sure to include your scale. Show and label your work.

4 in
4 in
4 in
3 in
3 in
3 in
4 in

Composting C-3                45

**Level 2**  The student demonstrated a partial understanding of the concepts and procedures assessed in the task. The student correctly labeled the base of the bin in the diagram for part *a*, but did not use the selected scale for both dimensions. The student did not find the volume of the bin.

---

**Bottom paper (Level 3):**

CHAPTERS 18-23

Name _____

### Building a Recycling Bin

Suppose you are going to build a recycling bin. The bin will have four congruent rectangular faces.

Each face will be rectangular in shape with dimensions of 3 ft in height and 4 ft in length.

a. You will build your bin on the top of a grassy area. Make a diagram that shows the shape and the dimensions of the base of your bin. Draw the dimensions to scale. Be sure to include your scale. Show and label your work.

½ in = 1 ft.

4 ft

4 ft

b. Make a scale drawing of the compost bin. Find the volume in feet of cubic/ your bin. Be sure to include your scale. Show and label your work.

½ in = 1 ft

Volume = l x h x w

4 ft x 3 ft x 4 ft = 48 ft³

Volume = 48 feet 3

width
4 ft

4 ft length
top 4 ft

3 ft hight
front
4 ft length

4 ft length
area
side
3 ft hight

Composting C-3                45

**Level 3**  The student solved all parts of the task correctly, and there was evidence of clear understanding of the concepts required in all parts. There was work to support all answers, and explanations were clear. The diagrams were accurate and enhanced the communication of the solution.

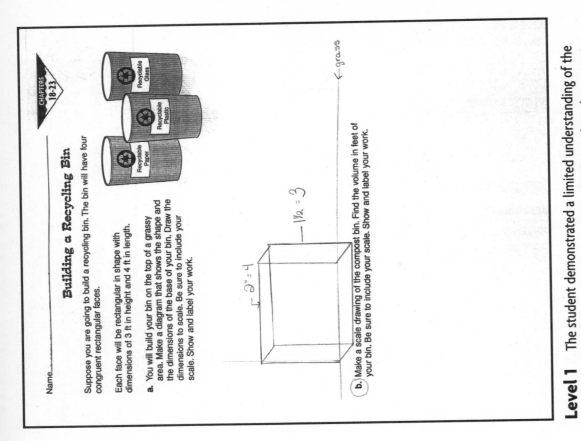

### Building a Recycling Bin

Suppose you are going to build a recycling bin. The bin will have four congruent rectangular faces.

Each face will be rectangular in shape with dimensions of 3 ft in height and 4 ft in length.

**a.** You will build your bin on the top of a grassy area. Make a diagram that shows the shape and the dimensions of the base of your bin. Draw the dimensions to scale. Be sure to include your scale. Show and label your work.

**b.** Make a scale drawing of the compost bin. Find the volume in feet of your bin. Be sure to include your scale. Show and label your work.

**TEACHER NOTES**

**Level 1** The student demonstrated a limited understanding of the concepts and procedures assessed in the task. The student drew a rectangular bin in the diagram for part *a*, rather than a diagram of the base drawn to scale. The student did not find the volume of the bin.

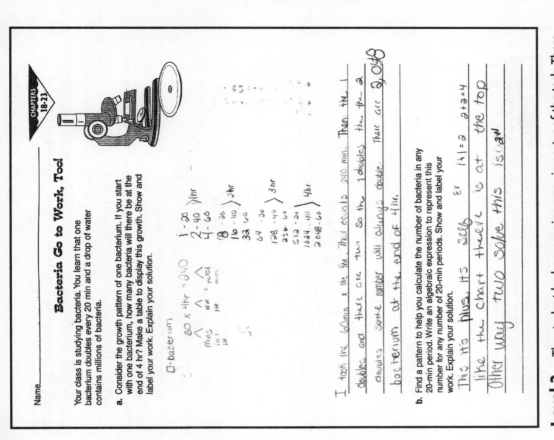

## Right paper (Level 2)

Name _____

### Bacteria Go to Work, Too!

Your class is studying bacteria. You learn that one bacterium doubles every 20 min and a drop of water contains millions of bacteria.

**a.** Consider the growth pattern of one bacterium. If you start with one bacterium, how many bacteria will there be at the end of 4 hr? Make a table to display this growth. Show and label your work. Explain your solution.

1-bacterium

$60 \times 4hr = 240$

| | |
|---|---|
| 1 - 20 | |
| 2 - 40 | }1hr |
| 4 - 60 | |
| 8 - 20 | }2hr |
| 16 - 40 | |
| 32 - 60 | |
| 64 - 20 | |
| 128 - 40 | }3hr |
| 256 - 60 | |
| 512 - 20 | |
| 1024 - 40 | }4hr |
| 2048 - 60 | |

I took the 60 min x the the that equals 240 min. Then the doubles and there are two. So the 1 doubles the the 2 doubles. Some number will always double. There are 2,048 bacterium at the end of 4hr.

**b.** Find a pattern to help you calculate the number of bacteria in any 20-min period. Write an algebraic expression to represent this number for any number of 20-min periods. Show and label your work. Explain your solution.

This its plus its self   ex  (4)=2  2+2=4
like the chart there is at the top
Other way two solve this is an

**Level 2**   The student had a reasoning error in part *a* of the task. There will be two bacteria at the end of 20 min, not one as shown in the chart. In part *b*, the student made a large jump from "the number plus itself" to the expression $2^n$. Some work and explanations were clear.

## Left paper (Level 3)

Name _____

### Bacteria Go to Work, Too!

Your class is studying bacteria. You learn that one bacterium doubles every 20 min and a drop of water contains millions of bacteria.

**a.** Consider the growth pattern of one bacterium. If you start with one bacterium, how many bacteria will there be at the end of 4 hr? Make a table to display this growth. Show and label your work. Explain your solution.

| min | bacteria |
|---|---|
| 0 | 1 |
| 20 | 2 |
| 40 | 4 |
| 60 | 8 | 1hr
| 80 | 16 |
| 100 | 32 |
| 120 | 64 | 2hr

| 140 | 128 |
| 160 | 256 |
| 180 | 512 | 3hr
| 200 | 1024 |
| 220 | 2048 |
| 240 | 4096 | 4hr

8192
16384
32768

**b.** Find a pattern to help you calculate the number of bacteria in any 20-min period. Write an algebraic expression to represent this number for any number of 20-min periods. Show and label your work. Explain your solution.

$2^n$   power   n = # of 20-min period

$2^9$ power = 512   as your can

See at the end of the third hour.

**Level 3**   The student demonstrated understanding of all the key concepts required to solve this task. Using a table to determine the number of bacteria was a workable procedure for part *a*. In part *b* the student identified an algebraic expression and there gave an effective explanation.

## Bacteria Go to Work, Too!

Name _____

CHAPTERS
18-23

Your class is studying bacteria. You learn that one bacterium doubles every 20 min and a drop of water contains millions of bacteria.

**a.** Consider the growth pattern of one bacterium. If you start with one bacterium, how many bacteria will there be at the end of 4 hr? Make a table to display this growth. Show and label your work. Explain your solution.

| hour | Bacteria |
| --- | --- |
| 1 | 8 |
| 2 | 64 |
| 3 | 512 |
| 4 | 4096 |
| 5 | |
| 6 | |
| 7 | |
| 8 | |
| 9 | |

$8 \cdot 8 \cdot 8$

At the end of 4 hours you will have 4096 bacteria

**b.** Find a pattern to help you calculate the number of bacteria in any 20-min period. Write an algebraic expression to represent this number for any number of 20-min periods. Show and label your work. Explain your solution.

**Level 1** The student did not demonstrate understanding of the key concepts or procedures being assessed in this task. While the student did have the correct answer in part *a*, there was no evidence to support the answer. The student did not attempt to find a solution to part *b* of the task.

## TEACHER NOTES

# Dominoes

## Purpose
To assess student performance after completing Chapters 24–28.

## Materials
cm ruler

## Time
15 to 20 minutes per task

## Grouping
Individuals or partners

## Overview
Explain to students that this performance assessment is about dominoes. Each task is about drawing diagrams of dominoes, finding the amount of material needed to make dominoes, displaying dominoes, or purchasing dominoes.

### Task D-1   Really Big Dominoes for Little Kids
Students are asked to draw and label a diagram of a domino that is twice as long on all edges as a regular size domino. Then they draw a diagram of a box to hold these larger dominoes and determine the amount of cardboard needed to make the box.

### Task D-2   Triple Dominoes
Students are asked to draw, label, and find the surface area of a triple domino, based on the given dimensions. Then they determine the amount of material needed to make a set of 55 dominoes.

### Task D-3   Tumbling Dominoes
Students are asked to find the perimeter and the area of a table and then determine the number of dominoes needed to make a display if the dominoes are placed upright around the perimeter and along one diagonal.

### Task D-4   Jumbo Dot Dominoes
Students are asked to find the cost of a set of dominoes that are on sale for 15% off the regular price and the cost of two sets of dominoes that are on sale for 20% off the regular price plus a 7% sales tax. Then they use information about previous sales to decide the best time to buy.

# Dominoes

| Task | Performance Indicators | Observations and Rubric Score (One score per task) |
|------|------------------------|---------------------------------------------------|
| D-1 | _____ Multiplies the dimensions of the regular size domino by 2 to find the dimensions of the larger domino. <br><br> _____ Draws and labels a diagram of the larger domino. <br><br> _____ Designs a box to hold a set of 55 of the larger dominoes. <br><br> _____ Draws and labels a diagram of the box. <br><br> _____ Determines the amount of cardboard needed to make the box. <br><br> _____ Explains the solutions. | 3    2    1    0 |
| D-2 | _____ Draws and labels a drawing of a triple domino. <br><br> _____ Determines the surface area of the domino. <br><br> _____ Draws a diagram to show the amount of material needed to make a set of 55 dominoes. <br><br> _____ Explains the solutions. | 3    2    1    0 |
| D-3 | _____ Finds the width of the table top. <br><br> _____ Finds the area of the table top. <br><br> _____ Finds the perimeter of the table top. <br><br> _____ Identifies the number of dominoes needed if they are placed around the perimeter and along one diagonal of the table top. <br><br> _____ Explains the solutions. | 3    2    1    0 |
| D-4 | _____ Finds the sale price of one set of dominoes. <br><br> _____ Finds the cost of the dominoes with sales tax added. <br><br> _____ Finds the sale price of two sets of dominoes and the cost per set. <br><br> _____ Explains how to make a decision on when to buy the dominoes. | 3    2    1    0 |

**Total Score** _____/12

# Really Big Dominoes for Little Kids

A game supply company wants to create large dominoes for pre-school children. The dimensions of regular sized dominoes are 5.0 cm by 2.5 cm by 0.9 cm.

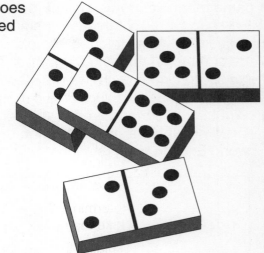

**a.** What are the dimensions of a domino that is twice as long on all edges? Draw a diagram, show, and label your work. Explain your solution.

_____

_____

_____

**b.** Design a box to hold a set of 55 of the larger dominoes. How much cardboard would you need to make your box? Draw a diagram of your box, show, and label your work. Explain your solution.

_____

_____

_____

Name_____

# Triple Dominoes

A game manufacturer is making a new triple domino in the shape of a rectangular prism as shown. The manufacturer wants to cut a sample domino from a piece of material that is 0.5 cm thick. Each section of the triple domino is 2 cm wide by 2 cm long.

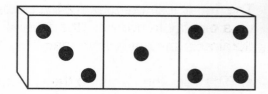

**a.** What is the surface area of the domino including the bottom? Draw and label a diagram of the domino. Show and label your work. Explain your solution.

_____

_____

_____

**b.** The manufacturer will cut out sets of dominoes from a reel of 12-cm wide material. Using the size of the domino from part **a**, how long a piece of material does the manufacturer need for each set of 55 dominoes? Draw a diagram to show your solution. Explain.

_____

_____

_____

# Tumbling Dominoes

The Toy Shop has a set of tumbling dominoes. It wants to set up a display to promote the sale of the tumbling dominoes. Each domino in the set is 2 in. long, 1 in. wide, and 0.25 in. thick.

**a.** The Toy Shop sets up the domino display on a rectangular table that has a length of 80 in. and a diagonal of 100 in. What is the area and perimeter of the table that the Toy Shop will use? Explain your solution.

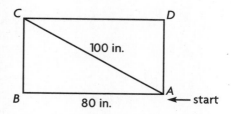

**b.** Toy Shop will place the dominoes upright on its narrowest edge around the perimeter and at a diagonal from one corner to the opposite corner of the table. How many dominoes will the Toy Shop need if they place the dominoes 1 in. apart? Show and label your work. Explain your solution.

# Jumbo Dot Dominoes

A box of Double Nine Jumbo Dot Dominoes
sells for $9.99.

**a.** The set is on sale for 15% off the $9.99 price.
If the sales tax is 7%, how much will the jumbo
set cost? Show and label your work. Explain
your solution.

_____

_____

_____

_____

**b.** If two sets are bought, the customer gets a 20% discount. Include
the 7% sales tax. What is the cost per set? Show and label your
work. Explain your solution.

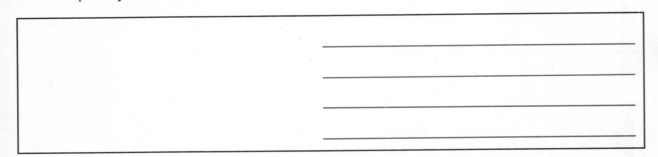

_____

_____

_____

_____

**c.** There are 10 Double Nine Jumbo Dot Dominoes sets left on the display table.
Your aunt wants to buy a couple of sets for gifts. It is 8:00 PM and the store will
have a midnight madness sale in just 4 hours. The dominoes will be 50% off. The
clerk tells you that 15 sets have sold since 10:00 AM. At the rate they have been
selling, should your aunt take a chance and wait until the sale or buy now? Show
how you arrive at your decision.

_____

_____

_____

_____

_____

_____

## Triple Dominoes

**CHAPTERS 24-28**

Name _____

A game manufacturer is making a new triple domino in the shape of a rectangular prism as shown. The manufacturer wants to cut a sample domino from a piece of material that is 0.5 cm thick. Each section of the triple domino is 2 cm wide by 2 cm long.

**a.** What is the surface area of the domino including the bottom? Draw and label a diagram of the domino. Show and label your work. Explain your solution.

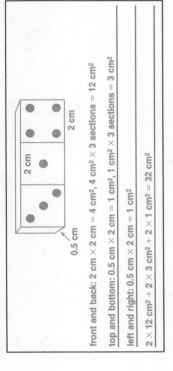

0.5 cm    2 cm    2 cm

front and back: 2 cm × 2 cm = 4 cm², 4 cm² × 3 sections = 12 cm²

top and bottom: 0.5 cm × 2 cm = 1 cm², 1 cm² × 3 sections = 3 cm²

left and right: 0.5 cm × 2 cm = 1 cm²

$2 \times 12 \text{ cm}^2 + 2 \times 3 \text{ cm}^2 + 2 \times 1 \text{ cm}^2 = 32 \text{ cm}^2$

**b.** The manufacturer will cut out sets of dominoes from a reel of 12-cm wide material. Using the size of the domino from part **a**, how long a piece of material does the manufacturer need for each set of 55 dominoes? Draw a diagram to show your solution. Explain.

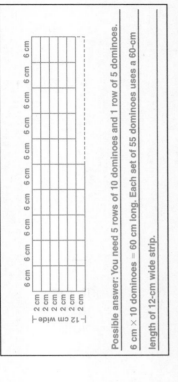

6 cm   6 cm   6 cm   6 cm   6 cm   6 cm   6 cm   6 cm   6 cm   6 cm

2 cm   2 cm   2 cm   2 cm   2 cm

12 cm wide

Possible answer: You need 5 rows of 10 dominoes and 1 row of 5 dominoes.

6 cm × 10 dominoes = 60 cm long. Each set of 55 dominoes uses a 60-cm length of 12-cm wide strip.

Dominoes D–2

60

---

## Really Big Dominoes for Little Kids

**CHAPTERS 24-28**

Name _____

A game supply company wants to create large dominoes for pre-school children. The dimensions of regular sized dominoes are 5.0 cm by 2.5 cm by 0.9 cm.

**a.** What are the dimensions of a domino that is twice as long on all edges? Draw a diagram, show, and label your work. Explain your solution.

5 cm    10 cm    1.8 cm

Possible answer: I multiplied the length, the width, and the height by 2 to find the new measurements.

**b.** Design a box to hold a set of 55 of the larger dominoes. How much cardboard would you need to make your box? Draw a diagram of your box, show, and label your work. Explain your solution.

11 × 1.8 cm = 19.8 cm ← height

5 × 5 cm = 25 cm ← length

10 cm ← wide

Possible answer: The dimensions of a box that would hold 5 stacks of 11 dominoes in each stack would have a height of 19.8 cm, a length of 25 cm, and a width of 10 cm.

19.8 cm = 11 × 1.8 cm

10 cm

$5 \times 5 \text{ cm} = 25 \text{ cm} \ (2\tfrac{1}{2} \text{ times length of } 10)$

Surface Area:
2 × (25 cm × 19.8 cm) = 990 cm²
2 × (10 cm × 19.8 cm) = 396 cm²
2 × (10 cm × 25 cm) = 500 cm²
990 cm² + 396 cm² + 500 cm² = 1,886 cm²

So, you need 1,886 cm² of cardboard.

Dominoes D–1

59

Name _____

## Jumbo Dot Dominoes

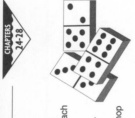
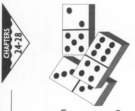

A box of Double Nine Jumbo Dot Dominoes sells for $9.99.

**a.** The set is on sale for 15% off the $9.99 price. If the sales tax is 7%, how much will the jumbo set cost? Show and label your work. Explain your solution.

> $9.99 \times 15\% = \$1.50; \$9.99 - \$1.50 =$
> $\$8.49; \$8.49 \times 7\% = \$0.59; \$8.49 +$
> $\$0.59 = \$9.08$
> Check student's explanations.

**b.** If two sets are bought, the customer gets a 20% discount. Include the 7% sales tax. What is the cost per set? Show and label your work. Explain your solution.

> $\$9.99 \times 2 = \$19.98; \$19.98 \times 20\% =$
> $\$4.00; \$19.98 - \$4.00 = \$15.98;$
> $\$15.98 \times 7\% = \$1.12; \$15.98 + \$1.12 =$
> $\$17.10; \$17.10 \div 2 = \$8.55$ per set

**c.** There are 10 Double Nine Jumbo Dot Dominoes sets left on the display table. Your aunt wants to buy a couple of sets for gifts. It is 8:00 PM and the store will have a midnight madness sale in just 4 hours. The dominoes will be 50% off. The clerk tells you that 15 sets have sold since 10:00 AM. At the rate they have been selling, should your aunt take a chance and wait until the sale or buy now? Show how you arrive at your decision.

> Possible answer: 10:00 AM to 8:00 PM = 10 hr; sold 1
> or 2 sets per hr in the past 10 hr. There are 4 hr until
> the midnight sale and 10 sets of dominoes left. If the
> sale pattern continues, the most the store will sell is
> 8 boxes. So there will be 2 boxes of Jumbo Dot
> dominoes left at midnight.

---

Name _____

## Tumbling Dominoes

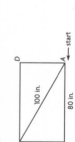

The Toy Shop has a set of tumbling dominoes. It wants to set up a display to promote the sale of the tumbling dominoes. Each domino in the set is 2 in. long, 1 in. wide, and 0.25 in. thick.

**a.** The Toy Shop sets up the domino display on a rectangular table that has a length of 80 in. and a diagonal of 100 in. What is the area and perimeter of the table that the Toy Shop will use? Explain your solution.

[diagram: rectangle with C, D top, B, A bottom; 100 in. diagonal; 80 in. width; "start" at A]

> $BC = 60$ in. and $AD = 60$ in.,
> perimeter is 60 in. + 60 in. + 80 in.
> + 80 in. = 280 in.,
> area is 80 in. $\times$ 60 in. = 4,800 in.$^2$
> Check students' explanations.

**b.** Toy Shop will place the dominoes upright on its narrowest edge around the perimeter and at a diagonal from one corner to the opposite corner of the table. How many dominoes will the Toy Shop need if they place the dominoes 1 in. apart? Show and label your work. Explain your solution.

> Possible answer: 60 in. $\div$ 1.25 in. = 48
> dominoes; 48 dominoes $\times$ 2 sides = 96
> dominoes; 80 in. $\div$ 1.25 in. = 64
> dominoes, 64 dominoes $\times$ 2 sides = 128
> dominoes; 100 in. $\div$ 1.25 in. = 80
> dominoes; 96 + 128 + 80 = 304 dominoes
> Check students' explanations.

# Model Student Papers for
# Dominoes

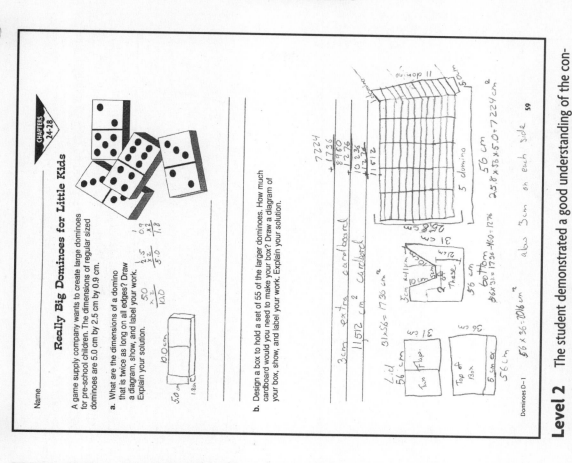

## Really Big Dominoes for Little Kids

A game supply company wants to create large dominoes for pre-school children. The dimensions of regular sized dominoes are 5.0 cm by 2.5 cm by 0.9 cm.

a. What are the dimensions of a domino that is twice as long on all edges? Draw a diagram, show, and label your work. Explain your solution.

b. Design a box to hold a set of 55 of the larger dominoes. How much cardboard would you need to make your box? Draw a diagram of your box, show, and label your work. Explain your solution.

Dominoes D-1

**Level 2** The student demonstrated a good understanding of the concepts and procedures assessed in the task. The student found the dimensions, drew, and labeled a diagram of the larger domino. In part, the student drew and labeled a diagram of the box, and made a good attempt at computing the needed cardboard.

---

## Really Big Dominoes for Little Kids

A game supply company wants to create large dominoes for pre-school children. The dimensions of regular sized dominoes are 5.0 cm by 2.5 cm by 0.9 cm.

a. What are the dimensions of a domino that is twice as long on all edges? Draw a diagram, show, and label your work. Explain your solution.

b. Design a box to hold a set of 55 of the larger dominoes. How much cardboard would you need to make your box? Draw a diagram of your box, show, and label your work. Explain your solution.

Dominoes D-1

**Level 3** The student successfully completed most parts of the task and gave evidence to support the answers. The diagrams were accurate and added to the reader's understanding of the solution. The student accounted for the extra cardboard needed to make a box that will hold all the dominoes.

**TEACHER NOTES**

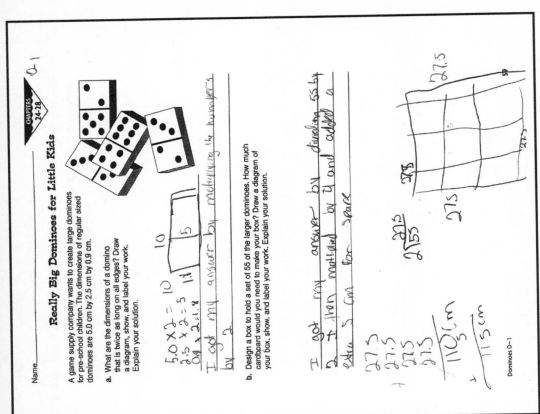

CHAPTERS
24-28

D-1

### Really Big Dominoes for Little Kids

A game supply company wants to create large dominoes for pre-school children. The dimensions of regular sized dominoes are 5.0 cm by 2.5 cm by 0.9 cm.

**a.** What are the dimensions of a domino that is twice as long on all edges? Draw a diagram, show, and label your work. Explain your solution.

5.0 × 2 = 10
2.5 × 2 = 5
0.9 × 2 = 1.8

10

5

I got my answer by multiplying 14 numbers by 2

**b.** Design a box to hold a set of 55 of the larger dominoes. How much cardboard would you need to make your box? Draw a diagram of your box, show, and label your work. Explain your solution.

I got my answer by dividing 55 by
2 then multiplied by 4 and added a
extra 5 cm for space

2)55
27.5

27.5
27.5
27.5
27.5
110 cm

115 cm

27.5

27.5

27.5

27.5

55

Dominoes D-1

**Level 1**  The student demonstrated limited understanding of the concepts and procedures assessed in the task. The student successfully completed part *a*. However, the work in part *b* showed no understanding of the concept of surface area.

## Level 2 (top)

Name _____

CHAPTERS
24-28

### Triple Dominoes

A game manufacturer is making a new triple domino in the shape of a rectangular prism as shown. The manufacturer wants to cut a sample domino from a piece of material that is 0.5 cm thick. Each section of the triple domino is 2 cm wide by 2 cm long.

a. What is the surface area of the domino including the bottom? Draw and label a diagram of the domino. Show and label your work. Explain your solution.

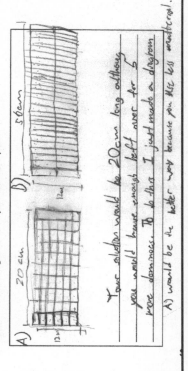

I found the area of each surface and added them all up.

b. The manufacturer will cut out sets of dominoes from a reel of 12-cm wide material. Using the size of the domino from part a, how long a piece of material does the manufacturer need for each set of 55 dominoes? Draw a diagram to show your solution. Explain.

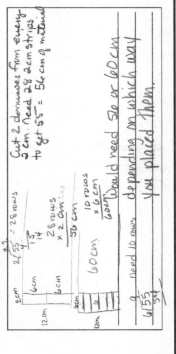

Your solution would be 20cm long although you would have enough left over for 5 more dominoes. To do that I just made a diagram.

A) would be the better way because it's less wasteful.

**Level 2** The student demonstrated a good understanding of the concepts and procedures assessed in the task. The student successfully drew and labeled the domino and determined the surface area. In part *b*, the student mislabeled the first diagram.

## Level 3 (bottom)

Name _____

CHAPTERS
24-28

### Triple Dominoes

A game manufacturer is making a new triple domino in the shape of a rectangular prism as shown. The manufacturer wants to cut a sample domino from a piece of material that is 0.5 cm thick. Each section of the triple domino is 2 cm wide by 2 cm long.

a. What is the surface area of the domino including the bottom? Draw and label a diagram of the domino. Show and label your work. Explain your solution.

Top      0.5cm x 6cm = 3cm²
Bottom                  3cm²
Back   2cm x 6cm =   12cm²
Front                  12cm²
Left  2cm x 0.5cm   1cm²
Right                  1cm²
Total                  32cm²

The surface area of each domino is 32 cm²

b. The manufacturer will cut out sets of dominoes from a reel of 12-cm wide material. Using the size of the domino from part a, how long a piece of material does the manufacturer need for each set of 55 dominoes? Draw a diagram to show your solution. Explain.

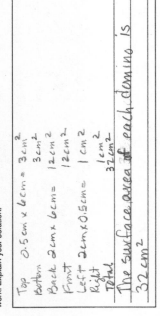

Cut 2 dominoes from every 2 cm. Need 28 2cm strips to get 55 = 56 cm of material

I need 10 rows.

Would need 56 or 60cm depending on which way you placed them.

**Level 3** The student demonstrated a clear understanding of the concepts and procedures assessed in the task. The student successfully labeled the given domino and determined the surface area. The student drew and explained two diagrams to show the amount of material needed to make a domino set.

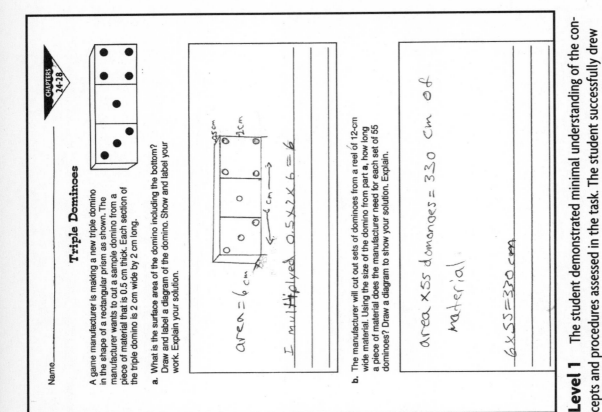

CHAPTERS
24-28

Name _____

## Triple Dominoes

A game manufacturer is making a new triple domino in the shape of a rectangular prism as shown. The manufacturer wants to cut a sample domino from a piece of material that is 0.5 cm thick. Each section of the triple domino is 2 cm wide by 2 cm long.

a. What is the surface area of the domino including the bottom? Draw and label a diagram of the domino. Show and label your work. Explain your solution.

area = 6 cm

I multiplyed 0.5 x 2 x 6 = 6

0.5 cm
2 cm
← 4 cm →

b. The manufacturer will cut out sets of dominoes from a reel of 12-cm wide material. Using the size of the domino from part **a**, how long a piece of material does the manufacturer need for each set of 55 dominoes? Draw a diagram to show your solution. Explain.

area x55 domonoes = 330 cm of
material

6 x 55 = 330 cm

**Level 1**   The student demonstrated minimal understanding of the concepts and procedures assessed in the task. The student successfully drew and labeled the domino, but was unable to find the surface area. In part *b*, the student made no attempt to draw a diagram.

## TEACHER NOTES

# Model Student Papers for
# Dominoes

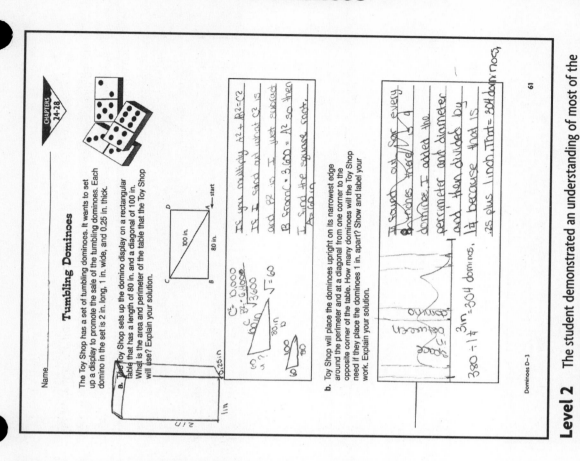

**Level 2**  The student demonstrated an understanding of most of the concepts and procedures assessed in the task. The student successfully found the width of the table using the Pythagorean Property, but did not show the area and perimeter of the table. In part *b*, the student used the correct perimeter.

**Level 3**  The student demonstrated accurate, complete, and clear understanding of the Pythagorean Property and finding perimeter and area. In part *b*, the student successfully found the number of dominoes and explained the strategies and procedures used.

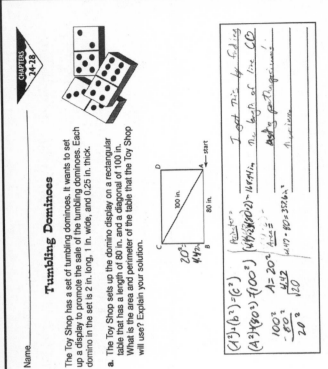

CHAPTERS
24-28

Name _____

### Tumbling Dominoes

The Toy Shop has a set of tumbling dominoes. It wants to set up a display to promote the sale of the tumbling dominoes. Each domino in the set is 2 in. long, 1 in. wide, and 0.25 in. thick.

**a.** The Toy Shop sets up the domino display on a rectangular table that has a length of 80 in. and a diagonal of 100 in. What is the area and perimeter of the table that the Toy Shop will use? Explain your solution.

C _____ D

20² | 100 in.
44² |

B ___ 80 in. ___ A ← start

$(A^2)+(b^2)=(c^2)$
$(A^2)+(80^2)=(100^2)$

$100^2$
$-80^2$
$\overline{20^2}$

Perimeter:
$(4)(20)+(80)(2) = 164.4$ in

Area =
$A = 20^2$
$\begin{array}{c}44^2\\ \overline{\sqrt{20}}\end{array}$
$4.47 \cdot 80 = 3526$ in²

I got this by finding the length of line CD
using Pythagorean Theorem.

**b.** Toy Shop will place the dominoes upright on its narrowest edge around the perimeter and at a diagonal from one corner to the opposite corner of the table. How many dominoes will the Toy Shop need if they place the dominoes 1 in. apart? Show and label your work. Explain your solution.

$168.94 = 169$ in
$+100$ in
$\overline{269}$ → 269 dominoes

I got this by adding the perimeter to the diagonal and figuring how many inches it was, which is the same as the amount of dominoes.

**Level 1** The student demonstrated minimal understanding of the concepts and procedures assessed in the task. In part *a*, the student attempted to use the Pythagorean Property but was not successful. In part *b*, the student did not understand that the dominoes were evenly spaced.

## TEACHER NOTES

## Paper 1 (Level 2)

CHAPTERS 24-28

Name _____

### Jumbo Dot Dominoes

A box of Double Nine Jumbo Dot Dominoes sells for $9.99.

**a.** The set is on sale for 15% off the $9.99 price. If the sales tax is 7%, how much will the jumbo set cost? Show and label your work. Explain your solution.

$$\frac{85}{100} \times \frac{x}{9.99}$$

proportion

$$\times \frac{85 \times 9.99}{100} = 8.49 \quad 8.49 \times .07 = 0.59 + 8.49 =$$

9.08 is all you are going to pay. I got that by

(figuring 85% you will pay and turning into proportion and adding the sales tax to get total) 9.08

**b.** If two sets are bought, the customer gets a 20% discount. Include the 7% sales tax. What is the cost per set? Show and label your work. Explain your solution.

$$\frac{80}{100} \times \frac{x}{19.98}$$

proportion

$$x = \frac{80 \times 19.98}{100} = 15.98 \times 0.7 = 1.18 + 15.98 = 17.10$$

sets

I did the same thing did on the first one only

I divided the price (19.99) and

got ½ of the price of 85.

**c.** There are 10 Double Nine Jumbo Dot Dominoes sets left on the display table. Your aunt wants to buy a couple of sets for gifts. It is 8:00 PM and the store will have a midnight madness sale in just 4 hours. The dominoes will be 50% off. The clerk tells you that 15 sets have sold since 10:00 AM. At the rate they have been selling, should your aunt take a chance and wait until the sale or buy now? Show how you arrive at your decision.

8 hrs = 15 sets        Yes she should

½ ÷ 4 = 7.5? 8 sets     wait till 12:00

**Level 2** The student solved parts *a* and *b* correctly and there was evidence of understanding of the concepts required in these two parts. There was a large gap for the reader in part *c* where the student said, "Yes she should wait," but did not give evidence to support this statement.

## Paper 2 (Level 3)

CHAPTERS 24-28

Name _____

### Jumbo Dot Dominoes

A box of Double Nine Jumbo Dot Dominoes sells for $9.99.

**a.** The set is on sale for 15% off the $9.99 price. If the sales tax is 7%, how much will the jumbo set cost? Show and label your work. Explain your solution.

$$8.49 = 9.99 \times .85 \quad \text{discount price}$$
$$+ .59 = 8.49 \times 0.7 \quad \text{sales tax}$$
$$\$9.08 = \text{total price}$$

**b.** If two sets are bought, the customer gets a 20% discount. Include the 7% sales tax. What is the cost per set? Show and label your work. Explain your solution.

$$\$15.98 = 19.99 \times 8 .80$$
$$1.12 \quad 15.98 \times 0.7 = 1.12$$
$$\$17.10 \quad \text{total price for 2 sets}$$

**c.** There are 10 Double Nine Jumbo Dot Dominoes sets left on the display table. Your aunt wants to buy a couple of sets for gifts. It is 8:00 PM and the store will have a midnight madness sale in just 4 hours. The dominoes will be 50% off. The clerk tells you that 15 sets have sold since 10:00 AM. At the rate they have been selling, should your aunt take a chance and wait until the sale or buy now? Show how you arrive at your decision.

10 hrs to sell 15 sets = 1.5 sets/hr

16 sets should sell by closing

should have some left at 12.

They would cost $5.00 a set plus tax

$5.00 × .07 = $.35   So she would

pay $5.35 a set after midnight

**Level 3** The student solved most parts of the tasks correctly. There was evidence of understanding of the concepts required in all parts. There was work to support all answers, and explanations were clear. The student demonstrated clear understanding of all key concepts and procedures.

Name _____

### Jumbo Dot Dominoes

**CHAPTERS 24-28**

A box of Double Nine Jumbo Dot Dominoes sells for $9.99.

Dominoes Dominoes Dominoes $9.99

**a.** The set is on sale for 15% off the $9.99 price. If the sales tax is 7%, how much will the jumbo set cost? Show and label your work. Explain your solution.

15% of 9.99 = $1.50

9.99
- 1.50
  8.40

7% of $10 = 59¢

  8.40
+ 0.59
  9.99

**b.** If two sets are bought, the customer gets a 20% discount. Include the 7% sales tax. What is the cost per set? Show and label your work. Explain your solution.

20% of 8.99 = 1.80

8.99
7.50
$7.19

**c.** There are 10 Double Nine Jumbo Dot Dominoes sets left on the display table. Your aunt wants to buy a couple of sets for gifts. It is 8:00 PM and the store will have a midnight madness sale in just 4 hours. The dominoes will be 50% off. The clerk tells you that 15 sets have been selling since 10:00 AM. At the rate they have been selling, should your aunt take a chance and wait until the sale or buy now? Show how you arrive at your decision.

**Level 1**  The student demonstrated limited understanding of the concepts and procedures assessed in the task. In part a, the student made a minor error when subtracting. In part b, the student did not complete the task. No attempt was made for part c. There was no explanation for any of the work.

**TEACHER NOTES**

# Performance Assessment

## Class Record Form

| School | Assessment A | | | | | Assessment B | | | | |
|---|---|---|---|---|---|---|---|---|---|---|
| **Teacher** | Task A-1 | Task A-2 | Task A-3 | Task A-4 | Total | Task B-1 | Task B-2 | Task B-3 | Task B-4 | Total |
| **NAMES**      **Date** | | | | | | | | | | |
| | | | | | | | | | | |
| | | | | | | | | | | |
| | | | | | | | | | | |
| | | | | | | | | | | |
| | | | | | | | | | | |
| | | | | | | | | | | |
| | | | | | | | | | | |
| | | | | | | | | | | |
| | | | | | | | | | | |
| | | | | | | | | | | |
| | | | | | | | | | | |
| | | | | | | | | | | |
| | | | | | | | | | | |
| | | | | | | | | | | |
| | | | | | | | | | | |
| | | | | | | | | | | |
| | | | | | | | | | | |
| | | | | | | | | | | |
| | | | | | | | | | | |
| | | | | | | | | | | |
| | | | | | | | | | | |
| | | | | | | | | | | |
| | | | | | | | | | | |
| | | | | | | | | | | |
| | | | | | | | | | | |
| | | | | | | | | | | |
| | | | | | | | | | | |
| | | | | | | | | | | |
| | | | | | | | | | | |

# Performance Assessment

**Class Record Form**

| School | | Assessment C | | | | | Assessment D | | | | |
|---|---|---|---|---|---|---|---|---|---|---|---|
| | | Task C-1 | Task C-2 | Task C-3 | Task C-4 | Total | Task D-1 | Task D-2 | Task D-3 | Task D-4 | Total |
| **Teacher** | | | | | | | | | | | |
| **NAMES** | **Date** | | | | | | | | | | |
| | | | | | | | | | | | |
| | | | | | | | | | | | |
| | | | | | | | | | | | |
| | | | | | | | | | | | |
| | | | | | | | | | | | |
| | | | | | | | | | | | |
| | | | | | | | | | | | |
| | | | | | | | | | | | |
| | | | | | | | | | | | |
| | | | | | | | | | | | |
| | | | | | | | | | | | |
| | | | | | | | | | | | |
| | | | | | | | | | | | |
| | | | | | | | | | | | |
| | | | | | | | | | | | |
| | | | | | | | | | | | |
| | | | | | | | | | | | |
| | | | | | | | | | | | |
| | | | | | | | | | | | |
| | | | | | | | | | | | |
| | | | | | | | | | | | |
| | | | | | | | | | | | |
| | | | | | | | | | | | |
| | | | | | | | | | | | |
| | | | | | | | | | | | |
| | | | | | | | | | | | |
| | | | | | | | | | | | |
| | | | | | | | | | | | |
| | | | | | | | | | | | |
| | | | | | | | | | | | |
| | | | | | | | | | | | |
| | | | | | | | | | | | |

# ► Evaluating Interview/Task Test Items

The interview/task test items are designed to provide an optional instrument to evaluate each child's level of accomplishment for each learning goal of the *Math Advantage* program. These items provide opportunities for children to verbalize or write about his or her thinking or to use manipulatives or other pictorial representations to represent their thinking. They test children at the concrete and pictorial levels, where appropriate, so that you can assess each child's progress toward functioning at the abstract level. The items will enable you to analyze the child's thought processes as they work on different types of problems and will enable you to plan instruction that will meet your children's needs.

You may wish to use these test items as you work through the content in the chapter to determine whether children are ready to move on or whether they need additional teaching or reinforcement activities. You may also wish to use these test items with children who did not successfully pass the chapter test to determine what types of reteaching activities are appropriate. These test items may also be used with students who have difficulty reading written material or who have learning disabilities.

The test items are designed to focus on evaluating how children think about mathematics and how they work at solving problems rather than on whether they can get the correct answer. The evaluation criteria given for each test item will help you pinpoint the errors in the children's thinking processes as they work through the problem.

A checklist of possible responses is provided to record each child's thinking processes. The Class Record Form can be used to show satisfactory completion of interview/task test items.

**Student's Name** _____

| TEST ITEM | EVALUATE WHETHER STUDENT |
|---|---|
| **1-A.1** *To classify and compare sets of numbers*<br><br>Classify each of the following numbers as a counting number, a whole number, an integer, or a rational number:<br><br>$5, 0, ^-8, 3\frac{1}{2}, 7.2$<br><br>Explain your classifications. | _____ classifies 5 as a counting number, a whole number, an integer, and a rational number.<br><br>_____ classifies 0 as a whole number, an integer, and a rational number.<br><br>_____ classifies $^-8$ as an integer and a rational number.<br><br>_____ classifies $3\frac{1}{2}$ and 7.2 as rational numbers.<br><br>_____ explains the classifications. |
| **1-A.2** *To understand rational numbers*<br><br>Give three other names for each of these rational numbers: 0.4 and $\frac{1}{2}$.<br><br>Name a rational number between them, and explain your method for finding it. | _____ names three other rational numbers for 0.4 (possible numbers: 0.40, $\frac{2}{5}$, $\frac{4}{10}$).<br><br>_____ names three other rational numbers for $\frac{1}{2}$ (possible numbers: $\frac{2}{4}$, $\frac{5}{10}$, 0.5).<br><br>_____ names a number between 0.4 and $\frac{1}{2}$.<br><br>_____ explains a method for finding the number. |
| **1-A.3** *To use percents to compare parts of figures*<br><br>Fold a rectangular piece of paper in half twice to form four sections. Explain what part of the rectangle represents 25% of the whole, what part represents 50%, and what part represents 75%. | _____ explains that one section represents 25%.<br><br>_____ explains that two sections represent 50%.<br><br>_____ explains that three sections represent 75%. |
| **1-A.4** *To write equivalent numbers using fractions, decimals, and percents*<br><br>Name a fraction, a decimal, and a percent for this ratio: 7 to 10. Explain the method you used for naming each. | _____ names $\frac{7}{10}$ as the fraction, 0.7 as the decimal, and 70% as the percent.<br><br>_____ explains how each number was named. |
| **1-A.5** *To make circle graphs using equivalent fractions, decimals, and percents*<br><br>Explain how you would make a circle graph to display this data.<br><br>Favorite School Lunch<br><br>Pizza   40%<br>Tacos   35%<br>Burgers   25% | _____ explains how to calculate the measure of each central angle, multiply the equivalent decimal or fraction by 360°.<br><br>_____ explains how to use a compass to draw a circle.<br><br>_____ explains how to use a protractor to draw each central angle. |

| TEST ITEM | EVALUATE WHETHER STUDENT |
|---|---|
| **2-A.1** *To use exponents and scientific notation to represent numbers*<br><br>Show two ways to represent 10,000 by using exponents. Then write 62,000,000 in scientific notation. Explain your methods. | _____ shows two ways to represent 10,000 with exponents (possible ways: $10,000^1$, $100^2$, or $10^4$).<br><br>_____ writes 62,000,000 as $6.2 \times 10^7$<br><br>_____ explains the methods used for each. |
| **2-A.2** *To express the same numbers in both binary and decimal systems*<br><br>Explain how you would use expanded form to write the binary number $11011_{two}$ as a decimal number. | _____ explains that in expanded form the number is written as follows: $(1 \times 2^4) + (1 \times 2^3) + (0 \times 2^2) + (1 \times 2^1) + (1 \times 2^0) = 16 + 8 + 0 + 2 + 1$.<br><br>_____ names the decimal number as 27. |
| **2-A.3** *To model square numbers and find square roots*<br><br>Draw a square array to represent $4^2$ and name the number. Then draw a square array to model $\sqrt{36}$ and name the number. | _____ draws a $4 \times 4$ array.<br><br>_____ names the square as 16.<br><br>_____ draws a $6 \times 6$ array.<br><br>_____ names the square root as 6. |
| **2-A.4** *To model repeated calculations or procedures numerically and geometrically*<br><br>Start with a number. → Multiply by 3. → Write the product.<br><br>Explain how you would use this iteration process to write the results of the first four iterations. Start with 5. | _____ explains what the iteration diagram means.<br><br>_____ names the results of the first four iterations as 15, 45, 135, and 405. |

| TEST ITEM | EVALUATE WHETHER STUDENT |
|---|---|
| **3-A.1** *To estimate and find sums and differences of whole numbers and decimals*<br><br>Estimate 3.89 + 6.23 + 4.95. Explain your method. | _____ chooses an appropriate method of estimating (such as rounding or finding a range).<br><br>_____ applies the method correctly.<br><br>_____ identifies the estimated sum as about 15 (found by rounding). |
| **3-A.2** *To estimate and find products and quotients of whole numbers and decimals*<br><br>Show and explain each step as you find the product: 4.5 × 3.04. | _____ regroups only when necessary.<br><br>_____ knows basic facts.<br><br>_____ aligns partial products correctly.<br><br>_____ places the decimal point in the product correctly.<br><br>_____ identifies the product as 13.68. |
| **3-A.3** *To use the order of operations to solve problems*<br><br>Explain how you would use the order of operations to evaluate $75 - 5^2 \times 2 \div (8 - 6)$. | _____ explains the order as parentheses → exponent → multiply → divide → subtract.<br><br>_____ gives the value as 50. |

| TEST ITEM | EVALUATE WHETHER STUDENT |
|---|---|
| **4-A.1** *To add and subtract fractions and mixed numbers and estimate sums and differences*<br><br>Explain how you would estimate $3\frac{1}{4} + 4\frac{7}{8}$. Then show each step as you calculate the exact sum. | (To estimate)<br><br>_____ chooses an appropriate method of estimating.<br><br>_____ applies the method correctly.<br><br>_____ uses mental math to estimate.<br><br>_____ identifies the estimated sum as about 8 (found by rounding to the nearest whole number).<br><br>(To calculate)<br><br>_____ writes equivalent fractions with the LCD for $\frac{1}{4}$ and $\frac{7}{8}$.<br><br>_____ adds the fractions and whole numbers.<br><br>_____ rewrites the sum.<br><br>_____ identifies the calculated sum as $8\frac{1}{8}$. |
| **4-A.2** *To multiply and divide fractions and mixed numbers*<br><br>Show each step as you find the quotient: $2\frac{1}{2} \div 3\frac{1}{8}$. | _____ writes the mixed numbers as fractions.<br><br>_____ uses the reciprocal to write a multiplication problem.<br><br>_____ uses the GCFs to simplify the factors.<br><br>_____ identifies the quotient as $\frac{4}{5}$. |
| **4-A.3** *To solve problems by **solving a simpler problem***<br><br>Explain how you could use the strategy **solve a simpler problem** to solve this problem. Then solve the problem.<br><br>Ali earned $4,500 last year. She put $\frac{1}{5}$ of her earnings in a savings account and spent $\frac{1}{3}$ of the remaining money on a stereo system. How much money did she spend on the stereo system? | _____ uses a smaller number ($45) instead of $4,500.<br><br>_____ computes with the smaller number:<br>$\frac{1}{5} \times 45 = 9 \leftarrow$ money saved<br>$45 - 9 = 36 \leftarrow$ money left<br>$\frac{1}{3} \times 36 = 12 \leftarrow$ cost of stereo system<br><br>_____ multiplies by 100 to get the actual cost of the stereo system.<br><br>_____ identifies the answer as $1,200. |

| TEST ITEM | EVALUATE WHETHER STUDENT |
|---|---|
| **5-A.1** *To add and subtract with integers*<br><br>Find the difference: $6 - {}^{-}3$. Explain your method. | _____ explains an appropriate method for finding the difference (modeling with counters or a number line, or writing a related addition expression: $6 + 3$).<br><br>_____ identifies the difference as 9. |
| **5-A.2** *To multiply and divide with integers*<br><br>Find the product: ${}^{-}5 \times {}^{-}3$ . Explain your method. | _____ explains that the product of two negative numbers is positive.<br><br>_____ identifies the product as 15. |
| **5-B.1** *To add and subtract with rational numbers*<br><br>Find the sum: $6.8 + {}^{-}2.4$. Explain your method. | _____ explains an appropriate method for finding the sum (same methods as for integers).<br><br>_____ identifies the sum as 4.4. |
| **5-B.2** *To multiply and divide with rational numbers*<br><br>Find the quotient: $\frac{-3}{4} \div \frac{1}{2}$. Explain your method. | _____ explains that the quotient of a negative number and a positive number is negative.<br><br>_____ identifies the quotient as ${}^{-}1\frac{1}{2}$. |

| TEST ITEM | EVALUATE WHETHER STUDENT |
|---|---|
| **6-A.1** *To write and evaluate numerical and algebraic expressions*<br><br>Explain what this expression means: $2(3n - 6) + 4$. Then explain how to evaluate the expression for $n = 3$, and give the value. | _____ explains that the expression means 3 times *n*, minus 6, multiplied by 2, and then added to 4.<br><br>_____ explains that you substitute 3 for *n* in the expression and follow the order of operations to evaluate it.<br><br>_____ identifies the value as 10. |
| **6-A.2** *To identify a pattern in a sequence and write an expression to describe it*<br><br>Write an expression to describe the sequence 5, 8, 11, 14, . . . Then use the expression to find the tenth term. Explain your method. | _____ writes $3n + 2$ as the expression to describe the sequence.<br><br>_____ identifies 32 as the tenth term.<br><br>_____ explains that, to write the expression, you<br><br>• find the common difference.<br>• write the product of a variable and the common difference as the first part of the expression.<br>• subtract the common difference from the first term and add the result to the first part of the expression.<br><br>_____ explains that, to evaluate the expression, you substitute the number of the term for the variable. |

| TEST ITEM | EVALUATE WHETHER STUDENT |
|---|---|
| **7-A.1** *To write equations for word problems*<br><br>Write an equation for this word sentence:<br><br>$12 less than the price of the CD player equals $195.<br><br>Then explain your equation and tell what the variable represents. | _____ writes the equation: $p - 12 = 195$ (*p* could be any letter)<br><br>_____ explains the equation.<br><br>_____ explains that the variable represents the price of the CD player. |
| **7-A.2** *To solve addition and subtraction equations*<br><br>Explain each step as you solve the equation $x + 4 = {}^-6$. Check your solution. | _____ subtracts 4 from each side of the equation.<br><br>_____ identifies the solution as ${}^-10$.<br><br>_____ checks the solution by replacing *x* with ${}^-10$. |
| **7-A.3** *To solve multiplication and division equations*<br><br>Explain each step as you solve the equation $3n = 51$. Check your solution. | _____ divides each side of the equation by 3.<br><br>_____ identifies the solution as 17.<br><br>_____ checks the solution by replacing *n* with 17. |
| **7-A.4** *To solve problems using the work backward strategy*<br><br>Explain how you could write an expression and use the strategy **work backward** to solve this problem. Then solve the problem.<br><br>Mark put some money in his wallet. He spent $4.50 for lunch and bought a book for $3.75. He had $1.75 left. How much money did Mark put in his wallet? | _____ writes the equation: $m - 4.50 - 3.75 = 1.75$<br><br>_____ solves the problem by using inverse operations to work backward:<br><br>$1.75 + 3.75 + 4.50 = m$<br><br>_____ identifies the answer as $10.00. |
| **7-A.5** *To identify, write, and solve proportions*<br><br>Explain each step as you solve the proportion.<br><br>$\frac{15}{5} = \frac{6}{a}$ | _____ writes the cross products $\rightarrow 15a = 5 \times 6$<br><br>_____ multiplies $\rightarrow 15a = 30$<br><br>_____ divides $\rightarrow \frac{15a}{15} = \frac{30}{15}$<br><br>_____ identifies the solution as 2. |

| TEST ITEM | EVALUATE WHETHER STUDENT |
|---|---|
| **8-A.1** To **write an equation** to solve a two-step problem<br><br>Explain how you could use the strategy write an equation to solve this problem. Then solve the problem.<br><br>The number of CDs that Megan has is 2 fewer than 3 times the number of CDs that Leon has. If Megan has 13 CDs, how many does Leon have? | _____ writes the equation $3x - 2 = 13$ to solve the problem.<br><br>To solve the equation:<br><br>_____ adds 2 to both sides:<br>$3x - 2 + 2 = 13 + 2$<br>$3x = 15$<br><br>_____ divides both sides by 3:<br>$\frac{3x}{3} = \frac{15}{3}$<br>$x = 5$<br><br>_____ identifies the solution as 5 CDs. |
| **8-A.2** To simplify and solve equations<br><br>Explain each step as you solve the equation $2(x + 4) + x = 17$. Check your solution. | _____ uses the distributive property:<br>$2x + 8 + x = 17$<br><br>_____ combines like terms:<br>$3x + 8 = 17$<br><br>_____ subtracts 8 from both sides:<br>$3x + 8 - 8 = 17 - 8$<br>$3x = 9$<br><br>_____ divides both sides by 3:<br>$\frac{3x}{3} = \frac{9}{3}$<br>$x = 3$<br><br>_____ identifies the solution as 3.<br><br>_____ checks the solution by replacing $x$ with 3 in the equation. |
| **8-A.3** To identify and find solutions to inequalities<br><br>Explain each step as you solve and graph the inequality $n - 2 < 3$. | _____ adds 2 to each side:<br>$n - 2 + 2 < 3 + 2$<br>$n < 5$<br><br>_____ identifies the solution as all numbers less than 5.<br><br>_____ draws a number line for the graph.<br><br>_____ shows an open circle at 5, with a ray extending from the open circle to the left. |

**Student's Name** _____

**Materials:** graph paper

| TEST ITEM | EVALUATE WHETHER STUDENT |
|---|---|
| **9-A.1** *To identify and graph ordered pairs on a coordinate plane*<br><br>Locate the point (2,⁻5) on a coordinate plane. Explain your method. | _____ explains that the first number tells how far to move horizontally.<br><br>_____ explains that the second number tells how far to move vertically.<br><br>_____ explains that for a positive number you move to the right or up.<br><br>_____ explains that for a negative number you move to the left or down.<br><br>_____ locates the point as 2 units to the right and 5 units down from the origin. |
| **9-A.2** *To identify and describe relations*<br><br>Explain each step as you make a mapping diagram and write an equation for this relation:<br><br>{(4,⁻8), (2,⁻6), (0,⁻4), (⁻2,⁻2), (⁻4,0), (⁻6,2)} | _____ explains that in the mapping diagram the numbers 4, 2, 0, ⁻2, ⁻4, and ⁻6 are in the domain, and that the numbers ⁻8, ⁻6, ⁻4, ⁻2, 0, and 2 are in the range.<br><br>_____ places numbers in the domain in one ring and numbers for the range in another ring and draws an arrow from each number in the domain to the appropriate number in the range.<br><br>_____ writes $y = {}^-x - 4$ as the equation. |
| **9-A.3** *To identify and describe functions*<br><br>On graph paper, draw a graph that represents a function and a graph that does not represent a function. Explain your choices. | _____ explains that a graph represents a function if no two ordered pairs have the same *x*-value (or if a vertical line crosses only one point on the graph).<br><br>_____ explains that a graph does not represent a function if two or more ordered pairs have the same *x*-value (or if a vertical line crosses two or more points on the graph).<br><br>_____ draws appropriate graphs. |
| **9-A.4** *To solve and graph linear equations*<br><br>Explain each step as you graph the equation $y = 2x$. | _____ makes a table of values.<br><br>_____ writes the solutions as ordered pairs.<br><br>_____ graphs the ordered pairs correctly. |

# Evaluation of Interview/Task Test

Date _____

**Student's Name** _____

**Materials:** dot paper

| TEST ITEM | EVALUATE WHETHER STUDENT |
|---|---|
| **10-A.1** *To determine whether plane figures are congruent and identify congruent line segments and angles*<br><br>On dot paper draw two line segments that are congruent. Then draw two angles that are congruent. Explain how you know that the figures are congruent. | _____ draws congruent line segments.<br><br>_____ draws congruent angles.<br><br>_____ explains that you can determine that figures are congruent by counting dots and spaces. |
| **10-A.2** *To identify line symmetry and rotational symmetry*<br><br>Identify the letters in the word **LINE** with these properties:<br><br>• line but not rotational symmetry<br>• rotational but not line symmetry<br>• both line and rotational symmetry<br>• neither line nor rotational symmetry<br><br>Explain your choices. | _____ explains that **L** has neither line nor rotational symmetry.<br><br>_____ explains that **I** has both line and rotational symmetry.<br><br>_____ explains that **N** has only rotational symmetry.<br><br>_____ explains that **E** has only line symmetry. |
| **10-A.3** *To identify and draw transformations of various figures and to graph figures on the coordinate plane*<br><br>On a coordinate plane, graph a triangle with vertices $A(0,0)$, $B(4,0)$, and $C(4,2)$. Draw a translation, a reflection, and a rotation of this figure on the coordinate plane. Explain how you drew each transformation. | _____ graphs the triangle correctly.<br><br>_____ draws a translation.<br><br>_____ explains that a translation occurs when the triangle is moved along a straight line.<br><br>_____ draws a reflection.<br><br>_____ explains that a reflection occurs when the triangle is flipped over a line.<br><br>_____ draws a rotation.<br><br>_____ explains that a rotation occurs when the triangle is turned about a point. |

Date _____

**Student's Name** _____

**Materials:** compass, straightedge

| TEST ITEM | EVALUATE WHETHER STUDENT |
|---|---|
| **11-A.1** *To construct congruent angles, and construct line and angle bisectors*<br><br>Draw an angle. Label the angle *ABC*. Explain each step as you construct the angle bisector. | _____ places the point of the compass at point *B* and draws an arc through ray *BA* and ray *BC*.<br><br>_____ draws intersecting arcs from the points on the rays where the original arc intersects the rays.<br><br>_____ draws a ray from point *B* to the point where the arcs intersect. |
| **11-A.2** *To identify, classify, and construct triangles*<br><br>Draw a triangle. Label the triangle *XYZ*. Explain each step as you construct a congruent triangle, *ABC*. | _____ explains the steps for constructing a congruent triangle by using the SSS rule, the SAS rule, or the ASA rule.<br><br>_____ uses the steps to construct a congruent triangle. |
| **11-A.3** *To construct parallel and perpendicular lines.*<br><br>Draw line *AB*. Choose any point *C* above line *AB*. Explain each step as you draw a line through point *C* that is parallel to line *AB*. | _____ explains the steps for constructing parallel lines.<br><br>_____ uses the steps to construct a line through point *C* that is parallel to line *AB*. |

Performance Assessment

**Student's Name** _____

**Materials:** dot paper or graph paper

| TEST ITEM | EVALUATE WHETHER STUDENT |
|---|---|
| **12-A.1** *To identify solid figures and their properties*<br><br>Name objects in the classroom or in your home that remind you of a rectangular prism, a pyramid, a cone, a cylinder, and a sphere. Explain your choices and tell whether each is a polyhedron or not. | selects appropriate objects for<br><br>_____ a rectangular prism.<br><br>_____ a pyramid.<br><br>_____ a cylinder.<br><br>_____ a cone.<br><br>_____ a sphere.<br><br>states characteristics to justify why objects were chosen for<br><br>_____ a rectangular prism.<br><br>_____ a pyramid.<br><br>_____ a cylinder.<br><br>_____ a cone.<br><br>_____ a sphere.<br><br>_____ identifies rectangular prism and pyramid as polyhedrons. |
| **12-A.2** *To solve problems by **finding patterns***<br><br>Explain how you could use the strategy *find a pattern* to solve this problem. Then solve the problem.<br><br>A triangular prism has 9 edges, a rectangular prism has 12 edges, and a pentagonal prism has 15 edges. How many edges does an octagonal prism have? | _____ explains that you can look at the pattern in the number of edges in the three given prisms (9, 12, 15, . . . ) or use the formula ($E = F + V - 2$).<br><br>_____ identifies the number of edges in an octagonal prism as 24. |
| **12-A.3** *To identify nets for solid figures*<br><br>Draw an arrangement of six squares that forms a net for a cube. Explain how you know the arrangement is a net for a cube. | _____ draws six squares that form a net for a cube.<br><br>_____ explains that if the arrangement were cut out and folded, it would form a cube. |
| **12-A.4** *To identify how to draw solid figures*<br><br>Explain each step as you draw a triangular prism on dot paper or graph paper. | _____ explains that you first draw the bases (triangles) one above the other.<br><br>_____ explains that you then draw line segments to make the lateral faces. |

**Materials:** dot paper or graph paper, scissors

| TEST ITEM | EVALUATE WHETHER STUDENT |
|---|---|
| **13-A.1** *To make and predict tessellation patterns*<br><br>Explain each step as you draw a quadrilateral on dot or graph paper, cut it out, and use it as a basic unit to make a tessellation of at least two rows. | _____ draws and cuts out a quadrilateral.<br><br>_____ traces the basic unit.<br><br>_____ explains how to place the basic unit next to the traced shape, without gaps or overlapping, to form a tessellation.<br><br>_____ make a two-row tessellation. |
| **13-A.2** *To identify visual patterns by changing positions or sizes of geometric figures*<br><br>Draw a square. Draw both diagonals in the square. Shade one of the four sections of the square.<br><br>Rotate the square 90° clockwise.<br><br>Explain each step as you complete the iteration process three times. Draw the figure at each stage. | _____ draws the figure.<br><br>_____ explains the iteration process.<br><br>_____ draws the figure correctly at each of the three stages. |
| **13-A.3** *To identify self-similarity in changing geometric figures*<br><br>Draw a square. Explain each step as you draw two stages of an iteration process of the square that have self-similarity. | _____ draws a square.<br><br>_____ draws two stages of an iteration process that show self-similarity.<br><br>_____ explains that the figures have self-similarity when the smaller parts at each stage are like the whole, except for size. |
| **13-A.4** *To build fractals by repeatedly changing geometric figures*<br><br>Explain each step as you complete the following iteration process two times for a square.<br><br>Draw a square. → Make one copy. → Reduce to half size. → Rebuild in bottom left corner. | _____ draws a square.<br><br>_____ explains the iteration process.<br><br>_____ draws Stages 1 and 2 of the iteration process correctly. |

| TEST ITEM | EVALUATE WHETHER STUDENT |
|---|---|
| **14-A.1** *To **draw a diagram** to solve problems using ratios*<br><br>Explain how you could use the strategy *draw a diagram* to solve this problem. Then solve the problem.<br><br>One model train can complete a lap of its track in 2 min. The other model train takes 3 min to complete a lap of its track. If the two trains start at the same time and run for 20 min, how many times will both be at the starting points of their tracks at the same time? | _____ draws a diagram to solve the problem. (possible diagram: number line showing numbers from 0 to 20 with multiples of 3 and multiples of 2 highlighted)<br><br>_____ identifies the answer as 3 times (after 6 minutes, 12 minutes, and 18 minutes). |
| **14-A.2** *To use rates, ratios, and proportions to compute unit rates and prices to solve problems*<br><br>Explain each step as you find the unit prices of these items. Tell which package has the lower unit price.<br><br>a 10-oz package of cheese for $1.79<br>a 16-oz package for $2.99 | _____ explains that you divide the price by the number of ounces to find the unit price of each package.<br><br>_____ identifies the unit prices as about $0.18 for the 10-oz package and about $0.19 for the 16-oz package.<br><br>_____ identifies the 10-oz package as having the lower unit price. |
| **14-A.3** *To use tables and graphs to show rates*<br><br>Look at the graph of taxicab rates on page 285. Explain what the data in the graph show and how you could use the data to determine the cost of a 6-mi taxi ride. | _____ explains that the graph shows that there is a $1.60 charge for the first $\frac{1}{8}$ mi and $0.20 for each additional $\frac{1}{8}$ mi.<br><br>_____ explains that the charge for the first mile is $3.00 and the charge for each additional mile is $1.60.<br><br>_____ identifies the charge for a 6-mi trip as $3.00 + 5($1.60), or $11.00 |
| **14-A.4** *To use proportions to identify the Golden Ratio*<br><br>Suppose line segment *AB* is 12 in long. Explain each step you would use to determine where to place point *C* on the segment to make a Golden Cut. | _____ explains that you would use the proportion $\frac{AB}{BC} = \frac{1.61}{1}$ (where *AB* = 12) to find the length of the Golden Cut.<br><br>_____ cross-multiplies to solve the proportion.<br><br>_____ identifies the distance from *B* to *C* as about 7.45 in. |

| TEST ITEM | EVALUATE WHETHER STUDENT |
|---|---|
| **15-A.1** *To change ratios to percents*<br><br>Explain each step as you write a percent for the ratio $\frac{17}{25}$. | _____ explains an appropriate method: writing an equivalent ratio that has 100 as the denominator ($\frac{17}{25} = \frac{68}{100}$) or writing and solving a proportion ($\frac{17}{25} = \frac{n}{100}$).<br><br>_____ uses the method correctly.<br><br>_____ identifies the percent as 68%. |
| **15-A.2** *To find the percent of a number*<br><br>Explain each step as you find 30% of 55. | _____ explains an appropriate method: changing the percent to a fraction or decimal and multiplying (55 × 0.3), writing and solving an equation (0.3(55) = $n$), or writing and solving a proportion ($\frac{n}{55} = \frac{30}{100}$).<br><br>_____ uses the method correctly.<br><br>_____ identifies the answer as 16.5. |
| **15-A.3** *To find what percent one number is of another number*<br><br>Explain each step as you find what percent 15 is of 25. | _____ explains an appropriate method: using a model and mental math, writing and solving an equation (25$n$ = 15), or writing and solving a proportion ($\frac{15}{25} = \frac{n}{100}$).<br><br>_____ uses the method correctly.<br><br>_____ identifies the answer as 60%. |
| **15-A.4** *To find a number when a percent of it is known*<br><br>Explain each step as you find the number when 6% of the number is 12. | _____ explains an appropriate method: using a model and mental math, writing and solving an equation (0.06$n$ = 12), or writing and solving a proportion ($\frac{12}{n} = \frac{6}{100}$).<br><br>_____ uses the method correctly.<br><br>_____ identifies the answer as 200. |

| TEST ITEM | EVALUATE WHETHER STUDENT |
|---|---|
| **16-A.1** *To identify similar figures and use scale factors to make similar figures*<br><br>Draw a rectangle with length 7 cm and width 4 cm. Explain how you would find the dimensions of a larger, similar rectangle with a scale factor of $\frac{3}{2}$. Draw the similar rectangle. | _____ explains that you need to multiply the measure of each side of the rectangle by the scale factor.<br><br>_____ draws the similar rectangle with length 10.5 cm and width 6 cm. |
| **16-A.2** *To use proportions to find unknown lengths of sides of similar figures*<br><br>Look at the triangles in Exercise 8 on page 326. Suppose you change the dimension on the larger triangle from 39 m to 52 m. Explain each step as you use a proportion to find the unknown length of the larger triangle. | _____ writes a proportion to find the unknown length: $\frac{52}{13} = \frac{x}{9}$.<br><br>_____ explains each step as the proportion is solved.<br><br>_____ identifies the unknown length as 36 m. |
| **16-A.3** *To use scale factors and proportions to relate area or volume of similar figures*<br><br>One cube has edges that are 3 cm and another cube has edges that are 6 cm. Name the scale factor relating the length of the edge of the larger cube to the length of the edge of the smaller cube. Explain how the surface areas of the cubes are related. Then explain how the volumes of the cubes are related. | _____ identifies the scale factor as 2.<br><br>_____ explains that the surface area of the larger cube is $2^2$, or 4, times as great as the surface area of the smaller cube.<br><br>_____ explains that the volume of the larger cube is $2^3$, or 8, times as great as the volume of the smaller cube. |

| TEST ITEM | EVALUATE WHETHER STUDENT |
|---|---|
| **17-A.1** *To use measurement and scale factors to draw similar figures*<br><br>Look at the triangle at the top of page 331. Explain each step as you use a scale factor of 2 to draw a similar triangle. | _____ uses a protractor to measure and record the angles of the triangle.<br><br>_____ multiplies the lengths of the sides of the triangle by 2 (the scale factor) to determine the lengths of the sides of the similar triangle.<br><br>_____ uses a ruler and a protractor to draw the sides and angles of the new triangle. |
| **17-A.2** *To read and make scale drawings*<br><br>Explain each step as you write and solve a proportion to find the actual distance if the map distance is 6.5 in. and the map scale is 1 in.:5 mi. Explain your method. | _____ explains that the proportion shows $\frac{\text{map distance}}{\text{actual distance}} = \text{scale}$, or $\frac{6.5}{d} = \frac{1}{5}$.<br><br>_____ solves the proportion.<br><br>_____ identifies the answer as 32.5 mi. |
| **17-A.3** *To use similar figures to measure lengths and distances indirectly*<br><br>Explain how you could use similar figures to help you solve this problem. Then solve the problem.<br><br>A tree casts a 12-ft shadow at the same time of day as a 30-ft flagpole casts an 8-ft shadow. How tall is the tree? | _____ explains how to use similar triangles to help solve the problem.<br><br>_____ writes a proportion to find the missing length (height of the tree): $\frac{12}{x} = \frac{8}{30}$.<br><br>_____ identifies the height of the tree as 45 feet. |

| TEST ITEM | EVALUATE WHETHER STUDENT |
|---|---|
| **18-A.1** *To use patterns to describe and extend triangular arrays*<br><br>Look at the array with Example 2 on page 358. What number will be repeated in Row 10? How many numbers will be in that row? What will be their sum? Explain your thinking. | _____ explains that you can use patterns to determine what numbers will be in each row.<br><br>_____ identifies 10 as the number repeated in Row 10.<br><br>_____ identifies 10 as the number of numbers in the tenth row.<br><br>_____ identifies $10^2$, or 100, as the sum of the tenth row. |
| **18-A.2** *To use patterns to determine how repeated doubling or halving affects positive numbers*<br><br>Explain each step as you determine how many times 3 must be doubled to reach or exceed 100. | _____ explains that you start with the number 3 and double it.<br><br>_____ explains that you continue to double the result until you reach a number equal to or greater than 100.<br><br>_____ identifies the answer as 6 times (3, 6, 12, 24, 48, 96, 192). |
| **18-A.3** *To use patterns in exponents and powers of numbers*<br><br>Explain each step as you find the first five powers of 4.<br><br>Start with 1. → Multiply by 4. | _____ explains that you start with 1 and multiply by 4 five times.<br><br>_____ identifies the first five powers of 4 as 4, 16, 64, 256, and 1,024. |

| TEST ITEM | EVALUATE WHETHER STUDENT |
|---|---|
| **19-A.1** *To use patterns to identify repeating decimals and to find a rational number between two rational numbers*<br><br>Rename $\frac{7}{15}$ as a decimal. Explain how you know whether it is a repeating or a terminating decimal. | _____ renames $\frac{7}{15}$ as 0.4666 . . . , or $0.4\overline{6}$.<br><br>_____ explains that the decimal is repeating because when you divide, the remainder is not zero. |
| **19-A.2** *To recognize and use patterns to find sequences in numbers, including positive and negative numbers and exponents*<br><br>Explain how you would write $4^{-5}$ by using a positive exponent and how you would write $\frac{1}{7^3}$ by using a negative exponent. | _____ explains that $4^{-5}$ rewritten with a positive exponent is $\frac{1}{4^5}$.<br><br>_____ explains that $\frac{1}{7^3}$ rewritten with a negative exponent is $7^{-3}$. |

| TEST ITEM | EVALUATE WHETHER STUDENT |
|---|---|
| **20-A.1** *To identify and use different types of samples and determine whether a sample is biased*<br><br>Is the following survey biased? Explain your thinking.<br><br>A manufacturer of backpacks wants to find out what color of backpack children aged 7–12 like best. They do a random survey of 250 boys aged 7–12. | _____ states that the survey is biased.<br><br>_____ explains that the survey is biased because only boys are surveyed.<br><br>_____ explains that an unbiased survey would include both boys and girls. |
| **20-A.2** *To identify appropriate questions and question types to use when collecting data*<br><br>Explain why the following question is not a good survey question. Give an example of a good survey question on this topic.<br><br>Is your favorite breed of dog a cocker spaniel, a poodle, or a golden retriever? | _____ explains that this is not a good question because it leads you to answer in only one of three ways.<br><br>_____ gives an example of a good question. (Possible question: What is your favorite breed of dog?) |
| **20-A.3** *To organize and display data (includes tally tables, frequency and cumulative frequency tables, and stem-and-leaf plots)*<br><br>Look at the data in the table in Example 3 on page 404. Explain each step as you make a line plot to display the data. | _____ explains the following steps:<br>• Draw a horizontal line.<br>• Put a scale of numbers (possibly 20, 25, 30, 35, 40, 45, 50, 55) on this line in equal intervals.<br>• Plot the data.<br><br>_____ displays the data on the line plot correctly. |

| TEST ITEM | EVALUATE WHETHER STUDENT |
|---|---|
| **21-A.1** *To determine how to show the distribution of a set of data*<br><br>Look at the histogram showing data about distances flown by paper airplanes at the top of page 411. Give:<br><br>• one statement about the distances you can tell from the data.<br>• one statement about the distances you cannot tell from the data.<br><br>Explain your choices. | _____ correctly states one thing about the distances that can be told from the data in the histogram. (Possible answer: Not many planes flew less than 170 in.)<br><br>_____ correctly states one thing about the distances that cannot be told from the data in the histogram. (Possible answer: whether any planes flew exactly 235 in.)<br><br>_____ explains the choices. |
| **21-A.2** *To choose an appropriate measure of central tendency to solve problems*<br><br>Explain each step as you find the mean, median, and mode for this set of test scores. Then explain which is a good measure of central tendency.<br><br>95   62   62   88   94   85 | _____ explains that the mean is the sum of the numbers divided by the number of addends in the group.<br><br>_____ explains that the median is the middle number when the numbers are ordered.<br><br>_____ explains that the mode is the number that occurs most often.<br><br>computes correctly:<br><br>_____ mean: 81<br><br>_____ median: 86.5<br><br>_____ mode: 62<br><br>_____ explains that the mean or the median is a good measure of central tendency. |
| **21-A.3** *To choose an appropriate graph to display data and identify how some graphs may be misleading*<br><br>What type of graph would you use to display each of the following?<br><br>• the heights of the students in your class<br>• the change in the high temperature each day during the past month<br><br>Explain your choices. | _____ chooses an appropriate type of graph for each. (Possible choices: heights—bar, histogram, or stem-and-leaf plot; temperature—line)<br><br>_____ explains that a line graph is most appropriate for showing changes over time. |

| TEST ITEM | EVALUATE WHETHER STUDENT |
|---|---|
| **22-A.1** *To use tree diagrams and sample spaces to determine possible outcomes*<br><br>Explain each step as you make a tree diagram to show the sample space for rolling a number cube with the numbers 1, 2, 3, 4, 5, and 6 and tossing a coin. | _____ explains how to construct a tree diagram correctly.<br><br>_____ shows 12 possible outcomes. |
| **22-A.2** *To find the probability of an event*<br><br>Suppose you roll a number cube labeled 1, 3, 5, 7, 9, and 11. Find P(multiple of 3). Explain your method. | _____ explains that the probability is the ratio of the number of favorable outcomes (two: 3 and 9) to the number of possible outcomes (six).<br><br>_____ identifies the probability as $\frac{1}{3}$. |
| **22-A.3** *To use the strategy* **make a list** *to find combinations, permutations, and the probability of specific outcomes*<br><br>Explain how you could use the strategy *make a list* to solve this problem. Then solve the problem.<br><br>There are 5 people getting on the bus. There are only 2 seats available on the bus. How many combinations of 2 people can be made from 5 people? | _____ makes an organized list to solve the problem.<br><br>_____ identifies the solution as 10 combinations. |

# Evaluation of Interview/Task Test

Date _____

**Student's Name** _____

## CHAPTER 23

**Materials:** coin

| TEST ITEM | EVALUATE WHETHER STUDENT |
|---|---|
| **23-A.1** *To find the experimental probability of an event*<br><br>Toss a coin 10 times. Record the results of your tosses. Explain how you can use the results to name the experimental probability of tossing heads. | _____ explains that the experimental probability is the ratio of the number of times the coin landed on heads to the total number of tosses.<br><br>_____ identifies the probability as $\frac{heads}{10}$. |
| **23-A.2** *To use random numbers to act out a probability experiment and design a simulation*<br><br>Look at the table of random numbers 1–5 on page 436. Explain how you could use the numbers in the table to solve this problem. Then solve the problem.<br><br>One out of every five tickets has a winning number. How many tickets will you have to buy to get two winning tickets? | _____ explains that you can use the numbers to do an experiment, or act it out.<br><br>_____ chooses a number (e.g., 1) to represent a winning ticket.<br><br>_____ counts how many numbers it takes to get two of the chosen number (e.g., two 1's).<br><br>_____ gives a reasonable answer (e.g., 15). |
| **23-A.3** *To find probabilities related to areas*<br><br>Look at the figure in Exercise 3 on page 454. Explain each step as you find the probability that a dart that hits the target will land in the white area. | _____ explains that the probability is the ratio of the area of the white border to the area of the entire figure.<br><br>_____ calculates the areas correctly.<br><br>_____ identifies the probability as $\frac{5}{6}$. |

Performance Assessment

# Evaluation of Interview/Task Test

Student's Name_____

Date_____

| TEST ITEM | EVALUATE WHETHER STUDENT |
|---|---|
| **24-A.1** *To determine the precision and greatest possible error of a measurement and to estimate length*<br><br>Explain each step as you find the smallest and largest possible actual length for a piece of ribbon that is marked 12 ft. | _____ explains that since the unit used is 1 ft, the greatest possible error is half of that, or $\frac{1}{2}$ ft.<br><br>_____ explains that to find the possible actual lengths for the measurement, you subtract and add the greatest possible error.<br><br>_____ identifies the actual length of the ribbon as $11\frac{1}{2}$ ft to $12\frac{1}{2}$ ft. |
| **24-A.2** *To use a network to find all possible routes and the shortest route*<br><br>Look at the network for Exercise 10 on page 471. Explain each step as you find all the possible routes between *C* and *A*, find the distance for each route, and name the shortest route. | _____ explains that there are three routes between *C* and *A*: *CA*, *CDA*, and *CBA*.<br><br>_____ identifies the distances as follows: *CA*: 45 mi; *CDA*: 52 mi; *CBA*: 50 mi.<br><br>_____ identifies the shortest route as *CA*. |
| **24-A.3** *To use the Pythagorean Property to find the length of the hypotenuse*<br><br>Explain each step as you use the Pythagorean Property to find the length of the hypotenuse of a triangle with legs 6 cm and 8 cm. | _____ explains that the Pythagorean Property is $a^2 + b^2 = c^2$.<br><br>_____ replaces the variables *a* and *b* with the lengths of the legs ($6^2 + 8^2 = c^2$).<br><br>_____ performs the operations correctly.<br><br>_____ identifies the length of the hypotenuse as 10 cm. |
| **24-A.4** *To use a formula to find the area of a parallelogram, triangle, circle, or trapezoid*<br><br>Explain each step as you find the area of a trapezoid with bases of 4 cm and 6 cm and a height of 8 cm. | _____ explains that the formula for the area of a trapezoid is $A = \frac{1}{2}h(b_1 + b_2)$.<br><br>_____ replaces the variables *h*, $b_1$, and $b_2$ with the appropriate lengths: $A = \frac{1}{2}(8)(4 + 6)$.<br><br>_____ performs the operations correctly.<br><br>_____ identifies the area as 40 cm$^2$. |

| TEST ITEM | EVALUATE WHETHER STUDENT |
|---|---|
| **25-A.1** *To find the surface area of prisms, pyramids, and cylinders*<br><br>Look at the prism in Example 1 on page 494. Find the surface area of the prism. Explain your method. | _____ explains that the surface area is the sum of the areas of the faces of the prism.<br><br>_____ identifies the surface area as 108 cm$^2$. |
| **25-A.2** *To find the volume of prisms, pyramids, cylinders, and cones*<br><br>Look at the cylinder in Exercise 1 on page 492. Find the volume of the cylinder. Then find the volume of a cone that has the same base and height as the cylinder. Explain how the volumes of these figures are related. | _____ explains that the volume of a cone is $\frac{1}{3}$ the volume of a cylinder with the same base and height.<br><br>_____ identifies the volume of the cylinder as about 125.6 m$^3$ and the volume of a cone with the same base and height as about 41.9 m$^3$. |

| TEST ITEM | EVALUATE WHETHER STUDENT |
|---|---|
| **26-A.1** *To determine how the area of a figure can change using a fixed perimeter*<br><br>Find the greatest possible area for a rectangle with a perimeter of 16 ft. Explain your thinking. | _____ explains that the rectangle with the greatest possible area is a square.<br><br>_____ identifies a square with 4-ft sides as the rectangle with the greatest possible area. |
| **26-A.2** *To use scaling to enlarge or reduce figures proportionately*<br><br>Explain how a rectangle 16 cm long and 10 cm wide is changed by these scale factors: Length, 75%; Width, 150%. Find the new dimensions and tell whether the perimeter and the area have increased or decreased. | _____ explains that in the changed rectangle the length is 75% of the length in the original rectangle and the width is 150% of the width in the original rectangle.<br><br>_____ identifies the new dimensions as a length of 12 cm and a width of 15 cm.<br><br>_____ determines that both the perimeter and the area of the rectangle increase. |
| **26-A.3** *To use a model to determine how the volume and surface area of a figure are affected by changing one or more of the dimensions of the solid figure*<br><br>Explain how the volumes and surface areas of a cube with a 3-cm edge and a cube with a 6-cm edge are related. Find the surface areas and the volumes of the two cubes. | _____ explains that the surface area of the larger cube is 4 times the surface area of the smaller cube.<br><br>_____ explains that the volume of the larger cube is 8 times the volume of the smaller cube.<br><br>_____ identifies the surface areas as 54 cm$^2$ and 216 cm$^2$, respectively.<br><br>_____ identifies the volumes as 27 cm$^3$ and 216 cm$^3$, respectively. |

Student's Name _____

| TEST ITEM | EVALUATE WHETHER STUDENT |
|---|---|
| **27-A.1** *To use proportions and percents to solve problems that involve finding sales tax, markups, and discounts*<br><br>Explain each step as you find the total cost of a jacket that has a regular price of $50 if the sales tax rate is 6%. | _____ explains that you either<br>• multiply the price by the sales tax rate to find the amount of sales tax and then add the amount of the sales tax to the price to find the total cost (50 × 0.06 = 3; 50 + 3 = 53), or<br>• multiply the price by 100% + sales tax rate to find the total cost in one step (50 × 1.06 = 53).<br><br>_____ identifies the total cost as $53. |
| **27-A.2** *To solve simple-interest problems*<br><br>Explain each step as you find the simple interest on $1,000 invested at 8% for 2 years. | _____ explains that the simple interest formula is $I = prt$.<br><br>_____ replaces the variables with the given values and calculates correctly.<br><br>_____ identifies the interest as $160. |
| **27-A.3** *To make a table to find interest paid on installment loans.*<br><br>Explain each step as you make a table to find the interest paid on an item that costs $75.50. The interest rate is 18% annually. Payments of $20 will be paid each month. | _____ finds the interest on the new balance after one payment.<br><br>_____ finds the balance with interest added in.<br><br>_____ finds the new balance with payment subtracted.<br><br>_____ identifies the interest as $1.62. |

| TEST ITEM | EVALUATE WHETHER STUDENT |
|---|---|
| **28-A.1** *To identify and describe relationships shown in pictures and graphs*<br><br>Look at the three graphs in Exercise 2 on page 551. Explain what each graph shows and describe a relationship that could be illustrated by each graph. | explains that<br><br>_____ graph *a* shows that as time increases, the distance increases.<br><br>_____ graph *b* shows that as time increases, the distance remains constant.<br><br>_____ graph *c* shows that as time increases, the distance decreases.<br><br>identifies appropriate relationships for<br><br>_____ graph *a*.<br><br>_____ graph *b*.<br><br>_____ graph *c*. |
| **28-A.2** *To show the relationship between two variables on a graph*<br><br>Identify the variables you would use to graph this relationship. Then explain how you would draw a graph to illustrate the relationship.<br><br>The greater the weight of a bag of oranges, the more it costs. | _____ identifies the variables as weight and cost.<br><br>_____ describes the graph correctly. |
| **28-A.3** *To show two sets of data on a scatterplot and identify their correlation*<br><br>Tell whether the variables would have a positive correlation, a negative correlation, or no correlation. Explain your thinking.<br><br>• the number of students in a school and the number of teachers<br>• a person's phone number and his or her weight<br>• the age of a used car and its value.<br><br>Then describe how the points on a scatterplot might look for each. | _____ explains that the number of students and the number of teachers have a positive correlation because the two sets of data increase at the same time; the points form a pattern that slants upward.<br><br>_____ explains that a person's phone number and weight have no correlation because there is no pattern relating the two sets of data; the points are scattered.<br><br>_____ explains that the age of a used car and its value have a negative correlation because as one set of data increases, the other set decreases; the points form a pattern that slants downward. |

# Performance Assessment

## Class Record Form • Page 1

**Teacher** _____

| | | | | | | | | | | | |
|---|---|---|---|---|---|---|---|---|---|---|---|
| 1-A.1 | To classify and compare sets of numbers | | | | | | | | | | |
| 1-A.2 | To understand rational numbers | | | | | | | | | | |
| 1-A.3 | To use percents to compare parts of figures | | | | | | | | | | |
| 1-A.4 | To write equivalent numbers using factions, decimals, and percents | | | | | | | | | | |
| 1-A.5 | To make circle graphs using equivalent fractions, decimals, and percents | | | | | | | | | | |
| 2-A.1 | To use exponents and scientific notation to represent numbers | | | | | | | | | | |
| 2-A.2 | To express the same numbers in both binary and decimal systems | | | | | | | | | | |
| 2-A.3 | To model square numbers and find square roots | | | | | | | | | | |
| 2-A.4 | To model repeated calculations or procedures numerically and geometrically | | | | | | | | | | |

# Performance Assessment

## Class Record Form • Page 2

Teacher _____

| | | | | | | | | | | | | | | | | | | | | |
|---|---|---|---|---|---|---|---|---|---|---|---|---|---|---|---|---|---|---|---|---|
| 3-A.1 | To estimate and find sums and differences of whole numbers and decimals | | | | | | | | | | | | | | | | | | | |
| 3-A.2 | To estimate and find products and quotients of whole numbers and decimals | | | | | | | | | | | | | | | | | | | |
| 3-A.3 | To use order of operations to solve problems | | | | | | | | | | | | | | | | | | | |
| 4-A.1 | To add and subtract fractions and mixed numbers and estimate sums and differences | | | | | | | | | | | | | | | | | | | |
| 4-A.2 | To multiply and divide fractions and mixed numbers | | | | | | | | | | | | | | | | | | | |
| 4-A.3 | To solve problems by solving a simpler problem | | | | | | | | | | | | | | | | | | | |
| 5-A.1 | To add and subtract with integers | | | | | | | | | | | | | | | | | | | |
| 5-A.2 | To multiply and divide with integers | | | | | | | | | | | | | | | | | | | |
| 5-A.3 | To add and subtract with rational numbers | | | | | | | | | | | | | | | | | | | |
| 5-A.4 | To multiply and divide with rational numbers | | | | | | | | | | | | | | | | | | | |

# Performance Assessment

## Class Record Form • Page 3

**Teacher** _____

| | | | | | | | | | | | | | | | | | | | | | | | | | |
|---|---|---|---|---|---|---|---|---|---|---|---|---|---|---|---|---|---|---|---|---|---|---|---|---|---|
| 6-A.1 | To write and evaluate numerical and algebraic expressions | | | | | | | | | | | | | | | | | | | | | | | | |
| 6-A.2 | To identify a pattern in a sequence and write an expression to describe it | | | | | | | | | | | | | | | | | | | | | | | | |
| 7-A.1 | To write equations for word problems | | | | | | | | | | | | | | | | | | | | | | | | |
| 7-A.2 | To solve addition and subtraction equations | | | | | | | | | | | | | | | | | | | | | | | | |
| 7-A.3 | To solve multiplication and division equations | | | | | | | | | | | | | | | | | | | | | | | | |
| 7-A.4 | To solve problems using the *work backward* strategy | | | | | | | | | | | | | | | | | | | | | | | | |
| 7-A.5 | To identify, write, and solve proportions | | | | | | | | | | | | | | | | | | | | | | | | |
| 8-A.1 | To write an equation to solve a two-step problem | | | | | | | | | | | | | | | | | | | | | | | | |
| 8-A.2 | To simplify and solve equations | | | | | | | | | | | | | | | | | | | | | | | | |
| 8-A.3 | To identify and find solutions to inequalities | | | | | | | | | | | | | | | | | | | | | | | | |
| 8-A.4 | To describe a sequence of numbers by writing an expression | | | | | | | | | | | | | | | | | | | | | | | | |
| 9-A.1 | To identify and graph ordered pairs on a coordinate plane | | | | | | | | | | | | | | | | | | | | | | | | |
| 9-A.2 | To identify and describe relations | | | | | | | | | | | | | | | | | | | | | | | | |
| 9-A.3 | To identify and describe functions | | | | | | | | | | | | | | | | | | | | | | | | |
| 9-A.4 | To solve and graph linear equations | | | | | | | | | | | | | | | | | | | | | | | | |

# Performance Assessment

## Class Record Form • Page 4

**Teacher**

| | | | | | | | | | | | | | | | | | | | | | | | |
|---|---|---|---|---|---|---|---|---|---|---|---|---|---|---|---|---|---|---|---|---|---|---|---|
| 10-A.1 | To determine whether plane figures are congruent and identify congruent line segments and angles | | | | | | | | | | | | | | | | | | | | | | |
| 10-A.2 | To identify line symmetry and rotational symmetry | | | | | | | | | | | | | | | | | | | | | | |
| 10-A.3 | To identify and draw transformations of various figures and graph figures on the coordinate plane | | | | | | | | | | | | | | | | | | | | | | |
| 11-A.1 | To construct congruent angles, and construct line and angle bisectors | | | | | | | | | | | | | | | | | | | | | | |
| 11-A.2 | To identify, classify, and construct triangles | | | | | | | | | | | | | | | | | | | | | | |
| 11-A.3 | To construct parallel and perpendicular lines | | | | | | | | | | | | | | | | | | | | | | |
| 12-A.1 | To identify solid figures and their properties | | | | | | | | | | | | | | | | | | | | | | |
| 12-A.2 | To solve problems by finding patterns | | | | | | | | | | | | | | | | | | | | | | |
| 12-A.3 | To identify nets for solid figures | | | | | | | | | | | | | | | | | | | | | | |
| 12-A.4 | To identify how to draw solid figures | | | | | | | | | | | | | | | | | | | | | | |
| 13-A.1 | To make and predict tessellation patterns | | | | | | | | | | | | | | | | | | | | | | |
| 13-A.2 | To identify visual patterns by changing positions or sizes of geometric figures | | | | | | | | | | | | | | | | | | | | | | |
| 13-A.3 | To identify self-similarity in changing geometric figures | | | | | | | | | | | | | | | | | | | | | | |
| 13-A.4 | To build fractals by repeatedly changing geometric figures | | | | | | | | | | | | | | | | | | | | | | |

# Performance Assessment

MATH ADVANTAGE
Grade 7

## Class Record Form • Page 5

**Teacher** _____

| | |
|---|---|
| 14-A.1 | To draw a diagram to solve problems using ratios |
| 14-A.2 | To use rates, ratios, and proportions to compute unit rates and prices to solve problems |
| 14-A.3 | To use tables and graphs to show rates |
| 14-A.4 | To use proportions to identify the Golden Ratio |
| 15-A.1 | To change ratios to percents |
| 15-A.2 | To find the percent of a number |
| 15-A.3 | To find what percent one number is of another number |
| 15-A.4 | To find a number when the percent is known |
| 16-A.1 | To identify similar figures and use scale factors to make similar figures |
| 16-A.2 | To use proportions to find unknown lengths of sides of similar figures |
| 16-A.3 | To use scale factors and proportions to relate area or volume of similar figures |
| 17-A.1 | To use measurement and scale factors to draw similar figures |
| 17-A.2 | To read and make scale drawings |
| 17-A.3 | To use similar figures to measure lengths and distances indirectly |

# Performance Assessment

## Class Record Form • Page 6

Teacher _____

| | | | | | | | | | | | | | | | | | | | | | | | | | | | | | | | | | |
|---|---|---|---|---|---|---|---|---|---|---|---|---|---|---|---|---|---|---|---|---|---|---|---|---|---|---|---|---|---|---|---|---|---|---|
| 18-A.1 | To use patterns to describe and extend triangular arrays | | | | | | | | | | | | | | | | | | | | | | | | | | | | | | | | | |
| 18-A.2 | To use patterns to determine how repeatedly doubling or halving affects positive numbers | | | | | | | | | | | | | | | | | | | | | | | | | | | | | | | | | |
| 18-A.3 | To use patterns in exponents and powers of numbers | | | | | | | | | | | | | | | | | | | | | | | | | | | | | | | | | |
| 19-A.1 | To use patterns to identify repeating decimals and to find a rational number between two rational numbers | | | | | | | | | | | | | | | | | | | | | | | | | | | | | | | | | |
| 19-A.2 | To recognize and use patterns to find sequences in numbers including positive and negative numbers and exponents | | | | | | | | | | | | | | | | | | | | | | | | | | | | | | | | | |
| 20-A.1 | To identify and use different types of samples and determine whether a sample is biased | | | | | | | | | | | | | | | | | | | | | | | | | | | | | | | | | |
| 20-A.2 | To identify appropriate questions and question types to use when collecting data | | | | | | | | | | | | | | | | | | | | | | | | | | | | | | | | | |
| 20-A.3 | To organize and display data (includes tally tables, frequency and cumulative frequency tables, and stem- and-leaf plots) | | | | | | | | | | | | | | | | | | | | | | | | | | | | | | | | | |

# Performance Assessment

## Class Record Form • Page 7

**Teacher**

| | | | | | | | | | | |
|---|---|---|---|---|---|---|---|---|---|---|
| 21-A.1 | To determine how to show the distribution of a set of data | | | | | | | | | |
| 21-A.2 | To choose an appropriate measure of central tendency to solve problems | | | | | | | | | |
| 21-A.3 | To choose an appropriate graph to display data and identify how some graphs may be misleading | | | | | | | | | |
| 22-A.1 | To use tree diagrams and sample space to determine possible outcomes | | | | | | | | | |
| 22-A.2 | To find the probability of an event | | | | | | | | | |
| 22-A.3 | To use the strategy *make a list* to find combinations, permutations, and the probability of specific outcomes | | | | | | | | | |
| 23-A.1 | To find the experimental probability of an event | | | | | | | | | |
| 23-A.2 | To use random numbers to act out a probability experiment and design a simulation | | | | | | | | | |
| 23-A.3 | To find probabilities related to areas | | | | | | | | | |

110

MATH ADVANTAGE
Grade 7

# Performance Assessment

## Class Record Form • Page 8

**Teacher**

| | | | | | | | | | | | | | |
|---|---|---|---|---|---|---|---|---|---|---|---|---|---|
| 24-A.1 | To determine precision and the greatest possible error of a measurement and estimate length | | | | | | | | | | | | |
| 24-A.2 | To use a network to find all possible routes and find the shortest route | | | | | | | | | | | | |
| 24-A.3 | To use the Pythagorean Property to find the length of the hypotenuse | | | | | | | | | | | | |
| 24-A.4 | To use a formula to find the area of a parallelogram, triangle, circle, or trapezoid | | | | | | | | | | | | |
| 25-A.1 | To find the surface area of prisms, pyramids, and cylinders | | | | | | | | | | | | |
| 25-A.2 | To find the volume of prisms, pyramids, cylinders, and cones | | | | | | | | | | | | |
| 26-A.1 | To determine how area of a figure can change, using a fixed perimeter | | | | | | | | | | | | |
| 26-A.2 | To use scaling to enlarge or reduce figures proportionately | | | | | | | | | | | | |
| 26-A.3 | To use a model to determine how the volume and surface area of a figure is affected by changing one or more of the dimensions of the solid figure | | | | | | | | | | | | |

# Performance Assessment

## Class Record Form • Page 9

Teacher _____

| | | | | | | | | | | | | | | | | | | | | | | | | |
|---|---|---|---|---|---|---|---|---|---|---|---|---|---|---|---|---|---|---|---|---|---|---|---|---|---|
| 27-A.1 | To use proportions and percents to solve problems finding sales tax, markups, and discounts | | | | | | | | | | | | | | | | | | | | | | | | |
| 27-A.2 | To solve simple interest problems | | | | | | | | | | | | | | | | | | | | | | | | |
| 27-A.3 | To make a table to find interest paid on installment loans | | | | | | | | | | | | | | | | | | | | | | | | |
| 28-A.1 | To identify and describe relationships shown in pictures and graphs | | | | | | | | | | | | | | | | | | | | | | | | |
| 28-A.2 | To show the relationship between two variables on a graph | | | | | | | | | | | | | | | | | | | | | | | | |
| 28-A.3 | To show two sets of data on a scatter plot and identify their correlation | | | | | | | | | | | | | | | | | | | | | | | | |

112